DATE DUE

OCT 2 , 1998

OCT 2 2 1998

NOV 1 9 1998

THE
BUSINESS KNOWLEDGE
REPOSITORY

THE
BUSINESS KNOWLEDGE
REPOSITORY

Consolidating and Accessing
Your Ways of Working

Jud Breslin and John McGann
Foreword by Bruce E. Bauman

QUORUM BOOKS
Westport, Connecticut • London

Library of Congress Cataloging-in-Publication Data

Breslin, Jud.
    The business knowledge repository : consolidating and accessing
your ways of working / Jud Breslin, John McGann ; foreword by
Bruce E. Bauman.
      p.   cm.
    Includes bibliographical references and index.
    ISBN 0–89930–484–2 (alk. paper)
    1. Re-engineering (Management)   I. McGann, John.   II. Title.
HD58.87.B74 1998
658.4'06—dc21   97–8857

British Library Cataloguing in Publication Data is available.

Library of Congress Catalog Card Number: 97–8857
ISBN: 0–89930–484–2

First published in 1998

Quorum Books, 88 Post Road West, Westport, CT 06881
An imprint of Greenwood Publishing Group, Inc.

Printed in the United States of America

The paper used in this book complies with the
Permanent Paper Standard issued by the National
Information Standards Organization (Z39.48–1984).

10   9   8   7   6   5   4   3   2   1

Contents

Illustrations

FIGURES

TABLES

Foreword

Bruce E. Bauman

In recent times, the business world has been almost obsessed with the subject of Business Process Re-engineering (BPR). Bookshelves are filled with an ever-increasing inventory of theories and approaches that will make business enterprise "lean and mean" and better able to compete in the "new world market." However, most re-engineering studies conducted by Fortune 1,000 companies end up being considered failures. They are viewed as such because they quite simply did not meet the expectations for efficiency and profitability set forth by their proponents.

Obviously, one might reasonably ask, What makes this book about Ways of Working different from those on business process re-engineering filling up a library's technical and business sections? The answer is quite simple. The authors are not attempting to convince you that re-engineering will solve all your problems, but they will show you a whole new way of understanding how *all* of your business enterprise works. A new reality, called Ways of Working, views re-engineering as a logical byproduct of the business process rather than some large independent project. You will not only learn why these "silver bullet" studies fail, but how easily an enterprise can define and communicate to all organizational and operational levels how work is currently done. The inclusion of all those involved with the company's work promotes an ongoing atmosphere of cooperation and enthusiasm for improving the Ways of Working of a business. Until now, most recommendations for change wound up not being implemented because they either represented a predetermined result, which will never accurately reflect the way you work, or were the result of some study, which is imposed on day-to-day workers without first seeking their counsel.

The authors have clearly illustrated how these massively expensive and time consuming re-engineering projects not only fail to reach their stated objectives, but often create an environment that is much worse than what existed before starting. With downsizing, re-organizing, and retrenching, the people absolutely necessary to develop better Ways of Working cannot help but view re-engineering as a threat to their continued employment. Worse yet, employees may have already left their jobs, thus creating a significant void of knowledge and experience. It becomes all managers and lower-level supervisors can do just to keep up with the routine and mundane tasks once performed by the day-to-day workers. When faced with the economic necessity to comply with external quality programs, such as GMP, ISO 9000, or QS9000 (currently mandated by the Big-Three auto manufacturers), the newly streamlined enterprise must now look outside for help to reach these objectives. It matters little in what industry one is involved in. FDA, OSHA, state insurance regulators, and bank inspectors can all have the same devastating impact on the daily routine of the enterprise.

To overcome this added burden, management has traditionally looked toward either its own information services people or, the true beneficiaries of this phenomenon, outside consultants. Neither of these entities is equipped to provide a proven framework to maximize profitability and productivity on a day-to-day basis. Even though claiming to start from existing procedures, in order to quickly accommodate additional external requirements, they will focus on only those business areas that seem absolutely necessary to meet complex new requirements. In addition, both internal and external consultants tend to have their own agendas, which are not always consistent with the actual needs of the business they serve.

Peter G. W. Keen, author, consultant, and educator, has made the observation that there is a big difference between getting a business process right and selecting the right business process to get right. Consultants and Information Systems people, he contends, look for those processes that best fit their own skill sets; that is, they select processes with many administrative steps, paper, and delays. These are not necessarily the best business processes for improved business performance at the bottom line.

Exponents of re-engineering now admit the failure to recognize the human element in the equation. We re-engineer where we are comfortable rather than where it is needed for improvement of the enterprise. Keen refers to a *Harvard Business Review* article that describes the experience of Mutual Benefit Insurance Company. This company re-engineered its policy processing system and cut the lapsed time required to issue an insurance policy from three weeks to one day; Mutual Benefit went Chapter 11 under state regulators; policy issuance was not the problem.

What Keen recommends is that we evaluate the processes in terms of worth (processes as invisible capital assets and liabilities) and salience (the importance to the corporate strategy). I would add the approach recommended herein allows the re-engineer to define more clearly how we do things so financial management can participate in the decision of which business processes are worthy and salient. Information services and outside consultants make decisions based on their unique agendas and particular skills and past experiences. This is why we say this book does not recommend re-engineering per se, but rather recommends a methodology to raise the decision-making process to a higher managerial level.

Without this overnight approach, the systems group will view every part of your Ways of Working with the narrow focus of how those ways are impacted by, or have an impact on, existing computerized systems. They will use data-flow diagrams, entity-relationship models, and action diagrams. These may be essential tools for information services to provide software and database designs, but they are normally confusing and ineffective vehicles for defining how work is performed within a business enterprise. We have all found ourselves attending presentations that first required a lesson on how to view the results of these tools. Even then, we were not totally comfortable in their use. Regardless of our comfort, none of those is intended to address work that does not involve computers. Manual and auxiliary off-site procedures are not accommodated.

The information services approach to problem solving blends a methodology to implement adequate systems with implementing the latest hardware and software techniques. Since the relative value of an individual in the information services world is normally tied to a list of technical accomplishments, the temptation to justify the next system upgrade or installation with one of these projects can be irresistible. Some have a difficult time recognizing their role as merely an organ within the corporate body rather than a prime reason for the company's existence. Their knowledge of the business they serve is often of secondary concern.

An employment advertisement that illustrates the previous point appeared in a prominent New Jersey newspaper. It said that responsibilities include designing and developing modifications to products and customer systems, formulating and defining system scopes through research and fact finding, and documenting and maintaining programs. COBOL, JCL, and VSAM experience is required. Additional experience with life insurance or the financial industry is a plus.

It is not bad enough that the technology sought after is not a leading edge. The fact that the insurance company views knowledge of the industry they serve as a footnote should be distressing to any insurance company CEO.

Consultants, on the other hand, are often motivated by billable hours. In addition, many of the largest consulting firms will set a dollar threshold that eliminates smaller potential customers from consideration. This book will discuss in detail an approach that some consultants will resist. This methodology places a premium on quickly and effectively communicating from top to bottom how your total organization goes about performing work. It is intended that the effort of capturing this wealth of knowledge be done only once, and that it include the practical experiences of those who actually do the work. Once the current Ways of Working have been identified as a baseline, proposed modifications to any level of work (called work objects) can be measured for savings in time and the associated cost.

Think about it. Every time a consultant walks through the door, the first thing he or she does is document current operating procedures. Each one documents work as an integral part of its individual engagement. The primary reason for this is obvious. In order to carry out an assignment, the consultant must develop specifications, for example, the specific assignment on which he or she is working. It does not matter whether the form is a pile of word processing documents, brown paper hung all over the wall with flow charts and notes on it, three-by-five cards stuck on the wall, or all these techniques. If the consultant is to address International Standards Organization (ISO) certification or develop a disaster recovery plan, he or she will document some small portion of the way you work. An auditor will also go about developing his or her own set of procedures documenting what you do and how you do it, and you end up with duplicate and costly documentation of what you know best anyway— the way you work.

What is more, some of the consulting firm's researchers have even less knowledge of your particular business, or even your industry, than your own resources. It is not uncommon to find your middle managers and lower-level supervisors having to explain the basics of some insurance principle or manufacturing concept to somebody billed out as an experienced and knowledgeable consultant. The redundant cost in both time and money can make the whole subject of process re-engineering impractical for a business, regardless of the anticipated benefits. More devastating, of course, is that this piecemeal, assignment-oriented approach never results in an overall view of how you work.

Horror stories abound about accepting and implementing a recommended solution. In the absence of any real knowledge of how *all* facets of a business actually work together, this can lead to financial and operational disaster. Here is a classic real-life example. A highly paid consultant recommended elimination of the purchasing requisition clerks in a high-tech firm. The clerks were downsized leaving the job of requisitioning supplies to over one thousand middle managers. The consultants calculated the savings of fifty clerks— over $1 million annually—and went home with their contingency fees. The company soon experienced severe bottlenecks bordering on total gridlock. Requisitions could not be processed. Soon routine orders for supplies evolved into critical demand. This was simple stuff—paper, pencils, erasers—things routinely ordered by the *former* clerical staff. The managers could not process requisitions which were, it was later determined, an accounting nightmare—they were trained inadequately. They were given manuals they could not read. They were resentful.

The lesson here is that re-engineering recommendations were not modeled nor reviewed "in the trenches." The answer may well have been to simplify first, then implement a true manager-oriented requisitioning process. On-line computer-based training and help desks would have avoided some of the pain. Our authors know that our Ways of Working approach could have helped this situation. One thing is certain, this recommendation failed because it was not part of a total and high-level solution. It was an independent consulting assignment designed to achieve a limited result.

What you are about to discover is a proven methodology which addresses the problems of developing an effective and, above all, workable set of recommendations for operational and organizational change. The key is communicating your enterprise's Ways of Working to and from the "trenches." This is a methodology that will insure success by allowing business process re-engineering to evolve from within rather than to complement procedures recommended from outside and mandated simply because of their excessive cost. The authors are not looking for, nor recommending, the hackneyed ownership of processes and procedures. What they *do* most strongly recommend is responsibility. Information services is responsible for any technology required, management for resources and support (commitment to attain success), and users are responsible for the successful operation of the improved process. Therefore, each must be completely involved, committed, and informed.

At the conclusion of this book you will absolutely understand how redefining your business process *can* be accomplished in a cost-effective manner. Real and practical improvements *are* attainable. Packaged software (preengineered) solutions *can* be implemented to completion, in a reasonable time frame, and at a predictable cost. Outsourcing (the ugly "O" word) part of your work *can* be evaluated as a viable alternative without the accompanying fear of losing control. The impact of technical systems recommendations *can* be jointly evaluated by information services and their nontechnical counterparts. The issue of the year 2000, with its date complications, can be addressed more cost effectively than now envisioned by Information Systems.

You will come to recognize and accept that better business strategies are now achievable; requisite technology is available, management will tune in, and users "in the trenches" can be brought into the fold. Together, this forms the basis for a new systems methodology. This practical and attainable repository of all your business processes is designed so you can overcome the ever-expanding demand for information about your Ways of Working. How to use the Ways of Working concept is the theme of this book. You will wonder why everybody isn't using it.

Preface

There is provable similarity between systems that address the same functions. Because of this, companies like Computer Associates can develop and market software packages to a myriad of diverse enterprises. To address the difficulties of implementing these generic systems into the diverse environments, software companies could develop system templates that detail and model the normal business practices inherent in manufacturing, distribution, human resource, financial, and banking software. The templates can be supported by development and modeling software used to create them initially so the end-users can modify these templates to reflect any unique use of the application software and to re-engineer and improve these processes. Finally, the underlying methodology must be in place to view these templates from any number of perspectives or "views" as done in the Ways of Working concept. This concept emerged in the late 1980s and resulted in one patent in June 1994.

Many software firms were exposed to Ways of Working. Some, including Computer Associates, Ross Systems, and Symix, adapted it as an implementation strategy. Others rejected it. It seemed that this was because these vendors believed manuals would suffice in assisting customers to understand the new systems and implement them successfully. As reported in this book, a vice president of a major financial institution suggested that software developers would respond to the user's needs only when the user demanded it. However, after dealing with software firms that do not provide adequate implementation tools and methodologies, observers conclude that many vendors simply do not understand the user or the user's needs that drive them to purchase software and develop computer systems. These developers are technicians who do not understand what a Ways of Working concept can achieve.

This author's conclusion was reinforced recently by an Atlanta-based vendor of distribution software. After a thorough review and exposure to the idea of templates, this vendor concluded the concept is "too sophisticated for our users." Yet, this vendor is marketing a $100-thousand distribution system, which it markets as "user-friendly." A major user has contacted this author to assist in a failed implementation. The technicians understand neither how their user base thinks nor its need to understand how distribution software works. This is the essence of the communications problem between software vendors and the clients to whom they sell their applications software.

A change has occurred recently. SAP, a major developer of manufacturing software, faced the reality that its R/3 system was difficult to implement. One magazine described it as powerful, expensive, and exhausting. In response, SAP management created an implementation toolset to assist its customer base. The Yankee Group, an independent information technology market research consultancy that specializes in helping users and vendors link their technology to their business strategy, recognized the significance of SAP's efforts and the existence of similar concepts such as Ways of Working. Advanced Manufacturing Research (AMR), a Boston-based think-tank, recognized the power of generic modeling and began development of a supply chain management model based on the Ways of Working concept. These efforts by certain leading-edge software vendors—SAP, the Yankee Group, and AMR—have given credibility to a concept that has been practiced by Computer Associates for six years and Ross Systems for two. The new tools will be marketed as systems implementation and application life cycle management systems. We refer to the concept tools and methodology as Ways of Working because we believe that if users can model their daily operations, easily modify them as circumstances change, with sophisticated graphics capabilities, they can improve systems, reduce implementation time and cost, and facilitate re-engineering of enterprise solutions.

These tools are coming into use because customers are demanding them. There is a growing group of forward-looking companies that have recognized the need for more rapid implementation and for more effective management and control of development of information systems.

Return on investment is a key issue that is at the core of the value of these tools. There are three features of the tools that allow them to provide both accelerated implementation and more rapid return on the company's information technology investment. First, the tools make all the business processes more visible. These processes represent all the relationships that companies need to model and understand within their company and within software solutions. Bringing those processes to the customer or the implementor, and making them more visible, means that both the customer and the implementation team can respond to what we call gap analysis. *Gap analysis* is the difference between what you would like to do and what the software "off-the-shelf" can do. Making processes more visible facilitates improvement and re-engineering of solutions.

Making processes more visible, in the Ways of Working context also means the ability to view processes from any number of perspectives. Once processes and procedures are defined accurately and in significant detail, users can view them through preestablished paths. For example, a process may be viewed as follows:

1. By function: "Show me how to enter a customer order."
2. By organization (and job description): "Show me any organizational responsibilities and my job description, which includes processing customer orders."
3. By index: "Customer orders."
4. By reinforced knowledge: "Define the process of entering customer orders."

In addition, making processes more visible means you can view them for different reasons or business strategies. As illustrated in Figure P.1, users may view the repository of business processes from various perspectives without change. For example, users may view a single critical process from an auditing perspective of internal controls, from a regulatory perspective for compliance, from a cost and timing perspective for potential re-engineering, or from a perspective of essential processing in the event of a disaster. Today, users may have each of these perspective views, but in most cases, they are separate, incompatible, and have been developed at great cost by separate specialized consulting efforts. Ways of Working is a single repository that eliminates the waste, duplication, and inaccuracy, and reduces the cost of maintenance of application systems.

Second, business engineering tools make the process of customizing software more manageable. After you have identified the changes that have to be made through gap analysis, the navigational and training capabilities of these business engineering tools can direct you much more efficiently to isolate what you have to customize and what you have to eliminate, what activities have to be done, and the resources necessary to handle those activities.

The third feature is that you can build "best practices" into the repository so that in a particular implementation you can share and understand the successes and failures from previous implementations. This is important from a multidivisional and a consultant's point of view. Big-Six firms, systems integrators, and other consultants could use these tools to leverage previous experiences that could be embodied in the repository to make each new implementation much more efficient than the last. The use of these tools should expand the use of best practices in the form of preconfigured templates such as AMR's template.

This toolset can also impact business process re-engineering. The trend has shifted from breaking things apart and looking for redundancies and waste to a trend of putting the pieces back together. Instead of just looking for what to eliminate, the movement is now focused on how to grow the system and the organization more efficiently. Business re-engineering can now be more proactive and focused on making the organization more efficient and better

FIGURE P.1
The Business Knowledge Repository: Viewing the Business
from Limitless Perspectives

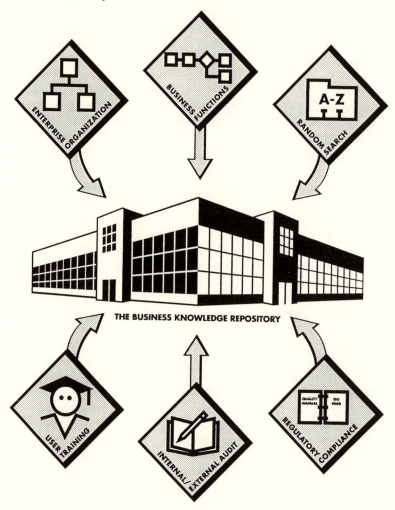

positioned to succeed. Re-engineering is enhanced and supported by defining your Ways of Working.

Michael Hammer has recognized this trend and the failures of earlier re-engineering efforts. When you read this book, you will learn why many re-engineering projects fail. Hammer recognizes this, and at a recent conference in Boston, he acknowledged that re-engineering is not about getting rid of people but about getting more out of people. You will read how Hammer launched a $4.7-billion re-engineering industry with his book on improving (e.g., re-engineering) business processes. In Boston, he stated that as he focused on engineering, which he now concludes is critical, he did not recognize human business knowledge sufficiently.

Companies that downsized, cutting staff for the sake of re-engineering, now recognize the same flaw; a lack of recognition of the human element that is the shortcoming of re-engineering books now on bookshelves. Many consultants are scrambling for new approaches and better data to support recommendations for business process improvements. They are trying to rethink their practices and are finally zeroing in on implementation of re-engineering approaches defined in this book and the concept of Ways of Working.

Changing how people work is not an easy proposition. But it is clear that it starts with understanding how they work and taking the time and effort to define it in detail, a process that we call Ways of Working. Some advocates of re-engineering site a search for something better as the allure of re-engineering wanes and horror stories mount. The term *re-engineering* is being dropped. To understand why, we would recommend that readers investigate research of leading-edge software vendors, including Ross Systems and SAP, and the observations of the Yankee Group and Advanced Manufacturing Research. At the same time, read this book, which is the something better that was missing from original re-engineering projects.

Hammer has expanded his educational practice to include more emphasis on the human element of proposed re-engineering projects. He stresses emphatically that downsizing is not re-engineering and acknowledged in the Boston conference, as reported in the *Wall Street Journal*, that front-line employees may be required to handle new and broader responsibilities. This book will give you a better way to accomplish this increase of responsibilities. It is a methodology supported by graphics software. Together they form a toolset and approach that defines our Ways of Working for the squeezed-out layers of management and the new front-line employees who need to "step up" or "step in."

Much of our initial research on these tools or toolsets focused on the issue of streamlining implementation, but these tools can be critical for re-engineering and for managing software and systems after they have been installed to improve business processes. That would include facilitating upgrades to the system and helping a company and its systems evolve. The toolset has to be, and is, focused on managing the life of the software and the human element of systems.

A valuable use of this concept will also occur in regulatory and standards compliance. It is based on the fact that the toolset provides a common repository for information representing both the business and the system. Because there is a common platform, because the knowledge is kept in one repository, because it is more visible to users, because a project management product is included with the tools—for all these reasons, it is natural that you can use them for ISO compliance or FDA approval. Some vendors have more fully-developed examples of the icons, but that is something this book will explore. We are describing not just templates for one particular industry but templates and functions that allow quality, government certification, re-engineering, and on-line training.

The Ways of Working concept provides views into a system. Users can take advantage of business engineering tools with systems that are running or were developed with life cycle management, to adapt the system for a change in business, or to add a new function to it. The concept will help manage upgrades as well.

This information engineering concept will be important in selecting new software and new vendors. In fact, it is as important as rapid implementation and life cycle management. It should be at the top of the requirements list. It will become more important, due to trends toward more user-configurable options, toward component-based solutions. If there are many more options that users can actually configure themselves, there is a need for tools to help them manage and understand those options. As software becomes more component-based, and users mix and match components from different vendors, tools are needed to help understand how components interact, how you interface to those components, how you map your business model into sets of components, and ultimately how you work.

Ways of Working is a forward-looking concept that recognizes that there is value in reviewing business processes, streamlining systems implementation, and improving life cycle management. It is now providing advantages to a group of visionary companies. This book is about this concept and these visionaries.

One such visionary is Ross Systems. Ross developed its implementation engineering concept under the name SAM—Strategic Application Modeler. The concept is important to Ross in increasing information solution value, simplifying information systems management, and reducing information solution cost of ownership. In regard to improving information solution value, a Ways of Working concept improves end-user productivity as well as the quality and value of business-process user communications.

In regard to the simplification of information services management, these new implementation and modeling tools provide viable and efficient maintenance of living system documentation in a single product. In addition, they support industry compliance standards, including both internal and mandated FDA standards, and facilitate business process change. Finally, in regard to reducing information solution cost of ownership, Ways of Working provides critical support for the rapid implementation methodology, reduces industry compliance and certification overhead, and ensures efficient business continuity. These observations, made by a real-life user of the best of these implementation tools, will be described, substantiated, and proven in the pages and chapters that follow.

The year 2000 provides an additional problem. Now information services is faced with the prospect of analyzing millions of lines of codes. We will contend in this book that Ways of Working, documentation from the user's perspective, is a better way to identify date problems and focus the source code search.

Introduction

Today enterprises must react to the need to maximize profits, streamline operations, and optimize productivity, employing approaches that have evolved over time. Today, users resort to business process re-engineering and mindless downsizing. The success rates of each—re-engineering and downsizing—have been historically disappointing. Re-engineering projects are a financial success for consultants but without many notable successes for the re-engineered. Downsizing can deprive companies of knowledgeable workers. It is often made possible by outsourcing work to firms that have acquired knowledgeable personnel from other companies that have downsized.

Re-engineered and downsized organizations find it is difficult to respond to emerging exigencies of day-to-day operations. They struggle with new external requirements, including the implementation of international quality programs such as ISO 9000, Big-Three automotive quality requirements of QS 9000, FDA-dictated quality regulations, OSHA dictates, society-driven need for disaster recovery plans, and the cost and necessity of external Big-Six audits. Just as companies thought the array of regulations was ending, ISO 14000 looms as the standard for environmentalists, and the problem of compliance will again be a challenge.

While business requirements and compliance need change, information technology is also changing. Client–server computing, which made sense twenty years ago, is being rapidly introduced. Yet, client–server computing requires a change in philosophy and operation. It requires different training, new development software, and sophisticated client communications. Trying to react aggressively to this change, while being required to implement and comply with state and federal regulations, strains the downsized leaner organization. Resorting to consultants has proved to be costly, since the necessary skills are in short supply. As this book will maintain, it is not the best use of strained financial resources nor the consultant's expertise. Then what is the answer? The answer lies in the need for a systematic blueprint of the information structure and the processes of doing business on a day-to-day basis. No framework exists to define the Ways of Working in an enterprise where processes cross divisional, organizational, and functional lines, as they inevitably do.

Engineers have blueprints and architects develop views. Accountants have accounting standards and a chart of accounts. Each addresses the specific need to know where we are and what our direction is. Corporate management in charge of planning change and defining new procedures in compliance with regulations, needs a similar framework and methodology to understand its Ways of Working. Requirements to maximize profits, streamline operations, and optimize productivity have two things in common: (1) the need to understand how things work now, and (2) the ability to effectively test different alternatives and only then implement changes to the current Ways of Working.

As discussed in the Preface, a group of forward-looking companies have adapted implementation tools that are based on the Ways of Working concept. Today, however, this framework or methodology is not widely used. Incredibly, companies retain one consultant to re-engineer processes, one consultant to implement ISO 9000 and all the regulations, one consultant to define disaster recovery plans, and a Big-Six firm to audit records. This approach assumes an organization does things differently for these different business necessities. It assumes there is no synergy between manufacturing systems and quality systems; between distribution systems and FDA regulations; and between normal operations and operations in cases of disaster, natural or otherwise.

This is not so. This book affirms the conclusion of commonality of processes and systems and develops a strategy wrapped in a framework, supported by a methodology. This is designed to put management in control of processes and processes into the forefront as the blueprints of change, the standard for all documentation, the basis for training, and the focal point for improved operations and competitiveness. As Joseph Sulewski, the technical director responsible for Ways of Working underlying software, said, "This is the only methodology and approach where the documentation is the system and the system is the documentation."

This book addresses communications between management which relies on information, end-users of computer applications which must use information, and the developers of applications; that is, the information services personnel and information services management. It addresses the need to infuse great amounts of management guidance and user knowledge and involvement (user power) in the enterprise strategy. It addresses the restructuring of current roles and relationships of management, systems designers, and end-users, encouraging analysts to apply their technical expertise to problem solving, and making users responsible for the definition of application systems and business processes that will meet their needs. It is about the scope of BPR with involvement of the key people—management, information services, and the end-user. It is about a methodology to use in structuring a new approach and it is a methodology that works. It is a framework for management to command the use of information by understanding the complexities of cross-divisional and cross-functional business processes, which we call the Ways of Working.

The problem is not new, but has been exacerbated as a result of downsizing. It has often been said that computer professionals do not adequately understand business problems and business users do not understand computers. Neither is comfortable with the long-term systems development life cycle, and management is displeased with the cost of obsolete systems, the long development cycle, the inability to respond to constant change, and the inevitable acrimony arising between users and the information services organization. At the same time, business processes can be old and entrenched and are not responsive to today's changing and more dynamic environment.

Every enterprise is searching for solutions that will make it more effective, more productive, more quality-oriented, and in cases of the private sector, more profitable. Approaches abound, but each has its complications and obstacles that must be overcome. For example, outsourcing of costly services, such as data processing, mailroom processing, and auditing is a strategy being investigated today. However, outsourcing calls for loss of control over the information services and data processing functions that may be vital to an enterprise. Even as a viable solution, many mangers reject outsourcing as a dangerous precedent. This option proposed by many has its complexities and challenging aspects and several dangers and potentials for failure such as the following:

- Inability to define and document the current situation and what the operation will produce. Will we be better off or worse?
- Inability to communicate effectively among the three key internal players: management, users, and Information Systems; and the one external player, the outsource consultant.
- Inability to define new systems requirements in a means understood by all, yet flexible enough to change as conditions change.
- Inability to get internal users in day-to-day operations (especially in a time of downsizing, cost cutting, and use of temporary employees) to cooperate effectively.

There are other options open to management to achieve increased productivity. Management can implement new preengineered (packaged) client–server manufacturing, financial, and distribution systems. New systems can be designed and implemented using the in-house information services staff. Outsourcing is an alternative. For each of these, a systematic review of current operations is required, and a methodical depiction of the current processes or Ways of Working should underlie each alternative. Review and improvement of each process is required. Therefore, business process re-engineering is not only an alternative approach, but a requisite and a prerequisite of all other potential Information Systems strategies.

The communications issue discussed is more important now than it was in the past. It is well recognized that information is vital today and that the power of information can make us more productive and can increase quality of operations, with the result that we become more competitive. In a time of intense international competition, companies are failing and jobs are being lost because of deficiencies in the use of information. To be more productive, improve quality, and therefore, be more competitive, we simply must get control over information. We must get the input of management and empower users so they can contribute to the information processing function. Governments and non-profit services are not immune; they too must communicate with users and develop a framework for understanding and managing processes.

Information Systems are the backbone of business processes, and business processes define how we do things, how well we produce, how well we compete, and how we can survive. These are our Ways of Working. Management cannot abdicate its role to manage vital Information Systems and resulting business processes. This was said over ten years ago in a book titled *Distributed Processing Systems: The End of the Mainframe Era?* At that time, we observed that mainframes were only going to survive in niche markets and that management was abdicating its role in anticipating reduction in the use of mainframes.

The reduction in centralized processing was slow in coming, but managers now take advantage of personal computing, graphics interfaces, and the new client–server environment. Distributed processing, described over ten years ago, is now a reality. We cannot wait another ten years to infuse management and users into the demise of old, obsolete, and poorly functioning systems and business processes.

Michael Hammer realized the importance of the business process (Ways of Working). Hammer, a former Harvard professor and highly regarded business thinker, has observed that the key to successful operations lies in business processes. These must be re-engineered to optimize the way we do business. He did recommend total replacement of processes, but has changed directions.

Others talk of customer-based systems and manufacturing. They are talking about the same thing, rethinking the systems process and re-engineering business processes to emphasize service and customer satisfaction. This, in turn, addresses issues of productivity, quality, and efficiencies of operation. Management must manage this effort, and users must export their knowledge into the end-product, or we will not produce customer-oriented processes.

Efforts are underway and several strategies have evolved. First, systems, in fact, are being redesigned, and the system development life cycle is being rethought. Second, software packages (preengineered applications) are common, and a healthy software development industry is in place. What is new here are better means of implementation and training that are now available, if not widely used. Third, some major players, such as Electronic Data Systems (EDS), Arthur Andersen, and Coopers & Lybrand, have established consulting practices specializing in re-engineering studies to improve processes. However, it will be clear that we believe that users should define and consultants should consult. Many large corporations are retaining consultants for large multimillion-dollar contracts. The problem, of course, is the cost and the knowledge base that is lost to the consultant. Fourth, the technology is being rethought by firms specializing in systems integration. Here high technology companies, such as CSC and Perot Systems, have consulting arms that analyze business processes and recommend technical solutions, such as local area networks (LANs) and wide area networks (WANs) to increase processing efficiencies at lower costs. Finally, the phenomena of outsourcing is growing in industries as diverse as banking and manufacturing. Kodak is a prominent example. Outsourcing is the process of turning over the information services process to a third party, such as IBM or ALTEL in Little Rock, Arkansas. The challenge here is to feel confident that the third party can perform as well or better than the in-house operation.

All these current strategies are aimed at improving and increasing productivity, cutting costs, and improving quality. Because this is critical, it demands attention from top management and the involvement of all who can make it happen; that is, not only the information systems staff, but also the neglected end-user and business analyst. The successful result will be a more competitive enterprise. It is simply a matter of who will manage the effort.

Management today is hungry for fresh ideas, too. This, on top of the information processing strategies discussed, might seem to complicate matters. But does it? Can't management's search be consistent, or at least complementary, to the information processing strategies? This should be possible since both information services management and operational management want to manage better and be more responsive to changing market conditions. The key to establishing synergy between management's approach and the various information processing approaches is the old bug-a-boo—communications and the need for a common framework to initially define, depict, and store the common practices or business processes as the Ways of Working.

Today, management is listening to the experts from high-level consulting agencies and academic institutions—and the advice is good. Peter M. Senge advocates using a learning organization where learning is central to success. We see this as management seeing the big picture, where failure to learn from experiences is untenable. Key to the learning organization is the iterative process of modeling one scenario and then another. This iterative process is a critical message in this book and a solution we see to today's information dilemma.

C. K. Prahalad of the University of Michigan calls for core competencies where we identify and organize around what we do best. Corporate strategies should be based on strengths that lead to several markets and are difficult for competitors to copy, according to this management strategy. Key to this strategy we believe, is the word "identify." How do we "identify" our core competencies so we can draw upon them?

David Nadler, a well-known consultant, recommends that management rethink the organizational structure in terms of how it works—how people and the informal structures interact. This, according to Nadler, leads toward groups and strategic alliances, which we are seeing daily in current business journals. Key to this relevant strategy is rethinking the organization and establishing alliances to fill gaps and establish competitive advantages.

George Stalks, Jr., another well-known consultant, advocates time-based competition where time is money. Time savings lead to improvements in quality, productivity, and, inevitably, competitiveness. Critical to this strategy is reduction in the cycle time, or the time it takes to complete a business process, such as getting an order to the manufacturing organization, fulfilling a customer order, or processing a customer invoice. In this strategy, management is urged to manage its own time as well as that of the enterprise. This strategy makes sense and works.

Business processes are the critical common element of all these examples— the learning organization, core competencies, organizational architecture, and time-based competition. The logic here is that each of the strategies, of necessity, requires an understanding of what we are doing now. What is the big picture, and how does the enterprise work (the learning organization)? What is the makeup of the organization, and who is responsible for what functions (the organizational structure)? What are our key strengths, and how do we maximize them (the core competencies)? What is our business process cycle, and what are the impediments that slow the outputs (time-based competition)? In each of these, the common thread is finding out what we are doing now, how are we doing it, who is doing it, and is there a better way? This is the very essence of a framework we call Ways of Working. Enterprises must define its Ways of Working and re-engineer or rethink each process before first, selecting a management strategy, and second, selecting an information services alternative to achieving that strategy. To us, it is consistent and logical and is the approach to achieving those elusive goals of cost-savings and improved productivity and competitiveness.

By defining our Ways of Working and re-engineering for each process, positive results are more feasible now than before. Why? Because these steps lead to new enlightened and technically aware management and the availability of a methodology and common sense approach to accomplish the task.

The technology is now available to define business processes. A methodology is also available to assure full communications among users, management, and information services, so all can contribute to the overall benefit of the enterprise—a very real framework can be provided for communication. The answer is clearer today than in the past because the technology has changed and the user is more sophisticated. The wall between users and information systems is crumbling. Information services will not argue that time is not available to experiment with new products and approaches. Past problems often resulted from poor communications. What is needed is to improve the ability of users and corporate management to plan and review what they want and adequately understand and control what is being developed. Today, there are many software products but a single methodology available to address the problems of miscommunication and to assist in the development of better business processes in a more productive and cost-effective manner, thereby addressing both problems of lack of productivity and quality. We refer to software tools to support the Ways of Working and to define functionality. There are tools to guide nontechnical personnel in defining and organizing data, modeling systems, prototyping business processes and procedures, generating meaningful reports, and ultimately, generating computer codes. Tools are available to control projects, graphically model processes, teach users online, and convert and control change to business processes—and they are available in an open architecture.

Yet in this sophisticated time of information processing, we are not always using what is available to help in the review of business processes. Project management software is not used to monitor the project. Documentation is manual on wall charts or in extensive narrative (word processing) that no one reads. Training remains in remote classroom settings or in on-line products not related to a company. Use of computerized training with relevant training software is minimal. Computer-aided software engineering (CASE) tools are used by less than 10 percent of computer sites here and abroad. Graphics, as part of CASE technology, are used even more sparingly. Yet, it is all available under an umbrella and methodology for defining our Ways of Working. Why are we not taking advantage of it?

The intriguing questions that arise from this situation, in fact, are a series of "whys":

1. Why does management no longer need to delegate its responsibility to manage, control, and maximize business processes to the information services group or to outside consultants?
2. Why do information services practitioners often neglect or resist the significant contribution that can be made by the user community?
3. Why are end-users not demanding more of a voice and a major role in the defining and re-engineering of business processes?

The answers to the first question may be apparent. Management is more technically skilled today and does not fear computing. Managers use computers, and new operating systems offer users easier access to software products. This has cut severely into the mystique that existed. It allows management to question and to pinpoint their strengths—that is, reviewing business logic, and when they are out of their element, for example, designing a LAN or WAN. It allows them, for the first time, to put technology use in perspective.

The answer to the second and third questions are more elusive, but it is clear that there still exists a communications problem between the information systems technician and the end-user, the final user of the system. The end-users, as a generalization, share the intimidation management did ten years ago. They, as well as management, must be ushered into the new era of PC awareness and assert their rightful role in the processes of improving the enterprise, such as the Japanese have done with quality circles and empowered users.

At the same time, the primary reason all available technology is not being used is a misunderstanding of how it can be used. Information systems practitioners struggle with new techniques for designing systems, the old systems development life cycle, and an uncertainty spawned by the ever-changing nature of the information systems function. Vendors may not help. More products are marketed, but there are few better solutions. Vendors promote classroom training that is ineffective. They produce manuals that nobody reads. We cannot keep up with the pace of products and literature, and we keep searching for the solutions.

What is needed is focus. We believe the focus should not be on technology, but on processes (Ways of Working). This refocusing will enhance users' abilities to plan and review what they want and to control what is being developed for them. This, in turn, will allow users to assume more of a role in design, and information systems to devote more time to technical considerations. Users should be ready to accept the responsibility. They should become more involved with the process of evaluating business processes and lead in coordinating with external consultants. Consultants should reassume their roles as experts, as they did earlier. They should provide a repository of solutions and new approaches. Information systems should be the conduit of technical avenues to achieve what is defined by users. Users, information services, and consultants should all work in harmony.

What is needed is a new, yet logical, framework and a management–user–information systems triumvirate for systems design, re-engineering, review, and development which encompasses entire business processes, whether they cross divisional or organizational lines. Evaluation, review, redesign, development, implementation, and training on day-to-day operations is a joint effort. A new systems development life cycle is possible where all contribute based on their expertise, using available technical solutions. A process should be put into place in which the user concentrates on the business process function with consultants, using their expertise to hone and streamline the process. Information systems should select the hardware and design the networks and protocols using the latest technology, and systems integrators should aid with equipment and communication challenges. Management should manage the project, including setting the goals and providing the resources, while measuring the results.

The only thing missing is a common framework and the basis for communications. To solve these problems, business process reviews and studies are often parceled out to consultants at large costs and not always with successful results. There is a better way—the Ways of Working.

In this book, we will show that without a new approach to systems and business processes, a new methodology, all the tools—including CASE tools—will not be successful. The obstacles will remain; re-engineering studies will be used unsuccessfully, discontent will continue, total quality will suffer, and we will not be as competitive. As one expert points out, we cannot drop tool technology into a typically chaotic information systems environment, for it will not be used.

What we offer here is an approach that promises to be a breakthrough because it is simple and aimed at management, users, and information systems. It uses existing, not future, technology and a common methodology focused on the Ways of Working. Users contribute, management stays apprised, information systems concentrates on its proper role, and systems are developed more efficiently, at less cost, with higher levels of quality, and in less time. Several alternative approaches, including those listed previously, become viable candidates to improve processes, cut cost, improve productivity, and increase global competitiveness. Management strategies, including ISO 9000, internal audits, and disaster recovery planning become implementable in the same enterprise.

Re-engineering can also be accomplished in-house in a cost-effective manner. Process improvements are attainable. Packaged software (preengineered) can be implemented more successfully. Outsourcing can be evaluated as a viable alternative without the accompanying fear of losing control. Systems integration recommendations can be evaluated for their impact by information systems personnel and with nontechnical counterparts sharing in the decision.

Why is this suddenly feasible? Because we now recognize that there are better business strategies available, requisite technology for using it, management that is attuned to it, and users who can be brought into the fold. It is the basis for a new systems methodology, a very practical and achievable business process repository that we refer to as Ways of Working, which is based on existing capabilities and products.

THE
BUSINESS KNOWLEDGE
REPOSITORY

1

Ways of Working

Since its beginning, the use of computing has evolved at such an amazing rate that it is difficult to portray the extent of changes during the past forty years or understand why some aspects of the use of computing have lagged behind. It is possible to open the doors provided for maintenance purposes, and step inside a UNIVAC used during the 1950s. While inside, you can process a problem that behemoth once performed on a battery-operated portable computer that can hold over 10,000 times as much data in its memory and solve problems about 10,000 times faster than the older device. The problem being solved, however, may have been analyzed and designed for both computers in the same manner. Very little is new in the process of designing or re-engineering systems and solving problems with the possible exception of CASE tools that very few information services departments use. The process of multiple interviews between a business user and computer analyst is still the accepted procedure. The goal is to describe the problem and prepare a requirements statement, so programs can be developed and tested, user instruction manuals can be written, people can be trained in a classroom environment, and the solution will certainly follow. These steps (1) often lead to misunderstandings, and (2) may have been taken, even though programmed solutions were available or could easily be provided by modifying a vendor software package to solve the problem. The analyst may have been unaware of the packaged solution or of techniques that are currently being introduced that make it easier to solve problems. Why? Because the packaged software today is poorly documented and hard to understand. Most software vendors are to blame for this situation. They will not change until users demand it.

Analysts may not be trained or accustomed to the idea of having a user act independently in describing a problem and designing or suggesting a solution to it. Improvements in application development methods, including most software preengineering products, have not focused on the need to extend product capabilities into the user environment. However, techniques based on software engineering tools have been developed, tested, and put into operation that make a new level of increased participation in application development possible for users.

We just heard a CASE seminar speaker say that users are not knowledgeable anyway. "Who said users know the answer?" he asked. The implication is that the information services professional with his tool kit of CASE products and myriad of data-flow diagrams methods is the answer to new and re-engineered systems. Most of the audience was not listening to this speaker. That was fortunate.

We believe that users want to review application solutions in relation to their needs and specify concepts, innovations, and modifications to make the application useful in their companies and in their jobs. Software tools should be available to them to describe and review information needs in a form that is both easy to use and helpful in defining and designing or re-designing application solutions. This is good for information services, too, because it means that in-house development may once again prove to be a viable alternative to packaged applications software.

Of course, the authors realize it is difficult to introduce change in a company that has inflexible procedures for application and development and older methodologies for solving problems with a computer. These methods have been introduced chiefly through projects initiated by information services years ago with the techniques that are now obsolete: the long systems development life cycle, for example; or the systems which information services never documented, or for which training became an ineffective afterthought.

New techniques are needed in the process of developing, refining, and implementing business applications because of the following:

- The increasing role that business users need to take in the development and use of information and computer technology.
- The increasing familiarity that many business users have with personal computing software; they are getting dangerous.
- The frustrations that user management feels with the information services organization over delays or problems in implementing new applications to meet current and ever-changing business needs.

There are many new tools that organizations may use to solve their problems. Spreadsheets, database packages, graphics, hypertext, and fourth-generation languages are all available. But, at this time, they are infrequently used to define new systems or re-engineer old ones. This indicates that major changes need to take place in the role of business users interfacing with information services. A shift of responsibility to users may occur in a number of corporations. It is the client–server environment and distributed processing that will cause a significant impact on the development process, and increase the need for users to describe requirements and design business systems.

CHANGE IN THE AIR

The changes in the development process or methodology will result primarily as users experiment with new techniques for improving the definition of systems and business process flows. Their involvement will affect both the way that requirements for applications are obtained and how development activities are carried out. The use of user-readable graphics, for instance, has brought about opportunities for users to become less encumbered with formal written descriptions of their needs and application requirements and to rely more on picture-oriented representations of their desired application systems. The unreadable data-flow diagrams designed only for information services professionals need not be thrust on innocent users who cannot read them.

Graphics representations can and should take the form of information flows, activity analyses, and prototypes that express how jobs are done—the Ways of Working. They should be job focused and show people tasks with both manual and automated procedures. The display screens can also show traditional and complex flow charts. We got away from flow charts years ago; we should not have done so. These and other diagrams that are available have allowed business users to describe and review their present and planned work and explain new requirements. Screens and reports can be defined and presented logically. The graphics presentations make use of a data dictionary, encyclopedia, or repository that keeps track of information on existing and planned systems and the use of data in them, and users will understand them.

Another technique that is logical in the design, re-engineering, and implementation of systems is hierarchy presentations and decomposition. This is the concept of beginning at a summary level with systems overviews and exploding down to finer levels of detail to the eventual screens—reports and formats—and "press the enter key." These visual aids and techniques for addressing, defining, and re-engineering business processes have been developed into the products for users that need to define our ways of working. They have provided a simpler and more comprehensive means for users to design and document what a business process should do in their enterprises. The new concept of definition and business process repository provides links from user-generated ideas to tools for analyzing the ideas further, such as CASE tools for information services, that can lead to the generation of code and new applications. Therefore, products—and the visual capability they provide—can be thought of as a new framework for communicating needs of business users and a new understanding between users and information services. That would be refreshing. The information services organization can use these products to support and keep track of user planning. The software that supports the visual capability, known as *templates*, can also be used as a means of providing information or automated assistance back to users to guide and inform them of the impact of their business plans and requirements as will be illustrated.

The concept is a new approach to application design and development that addresses all phases of the Systems Development Life Cycle (Cycle). It is intended to advance the cause of applications development, whether for purchased packages, systems developed in-house, or systems that have been modified by their users. The Ways of Working concept focuses on the business process to increase visibility about a new or redesigned process and to shorten the lengthy Cycle of the application development. It focuses on the design of the application or business process by automating and graphically illustrating the design in a manner understood by the management team, information services professionals, and the end-users. The design, at the same time, is in a format that naturally and logically leads to user documentation and training scenarios normally completed only as an afterthought. It includes conversion specifications and data tracking and results in the generation of code based strictly on the agreed upon design. An illustration of the concept is Figure 1.1.

The concept is simple and straightforward. The focal point is the business process based on a reusable design component, consisting of process flows, screens, and data elements. These are in the form of business process templates and are the design dictionary. Its construction is based on the following three basic premises of business processes:

1. The common functionality of systems.
2. The reusability of design.
3. The importance of user participation in the Cycle.

We store these templates as a design dictionary.

COMMON FUNCTIONALITY OF SYSTEMS

The core functionality of major applications systems is basically similar. Financial systems adhere to generally accepted accounting principles; manufacturing, distribution, and banking systems are based on industry accepted procedures and principles. This core functionality underlies the software applications industry in which common systems are sold to diverse companies in diverse industries (horizontal markets) and diverse companies in single industries (vertical markets). It is a compendium of generic systems functionality, graphically displayed, modifiable, and organized into a hierarchy of detail by application—it is reusable design.

FIGURE 1.1
New Framework for Communicating User Needs

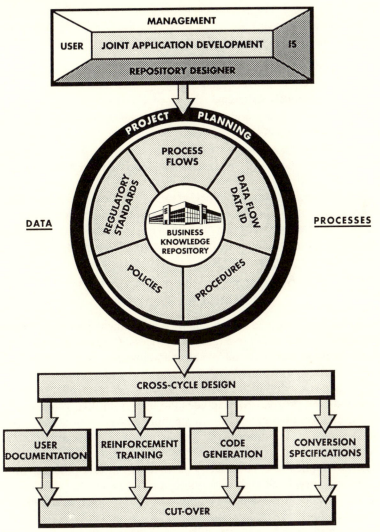

REUSABILITY OF DESIGN

Since the core functionality of major business processes is similar, the design functionality can be captured and retrieved. The Ways of Working is the design (reusable) components of the major functionality of financial, manufacturing, and distribution applications. It consists of the following three integrated components:

1. *Development Plan*: A detailed and automated plan to modify and enhance the design document and to document and train on each business process.

2. *Design Dictionary*: The detail documentation of the Ways of Working includes five levels of detail. They are
   - Summary clusters of like functions
   - Decomposition of the cluster into its logical components
   - Business functions and processes depicted as process flows
   - Procedures or work statements
   - Screen formats with data elements and edits, reports, forms, and other vehicles of data transmission

3. *Data Tracking*: The key data elements in each business process with its identification, size, attributes and directory, and full indexing capability.

The design dictionary is hierarchical, graphics oriented, and modifiable, but most important, it is easily understood by information services personnel, users, and the management team. This is because of the focus on processes and the use of easily understandable and modifiable graphic icons.

IMPORTANCE OF USER PARTICIPATION IN BUSINESS PROCESS

Users must be involved in the changes to business processes whenever organizations decide to (1) re-engineer a process, (2) develop a new system affecting business processes, or (3) select and implement a software package of business processes.

The Systems Development Life Cycle on each has historically been a long and phase-driven process that excludes the user from involvement after the initial requirements statement, or in some more advanced environments, after the general design. The information services staff traditionally goes behind closed doors to write a detail design, prepare program specifications, code, and test the application. The user is excluded from this process, which is technical and completed with methodologies that he or she does not understand. This results in misunderstandings and systems that do not reflect the original user intent or requirements.

The new approach to systems, whether packaged, designed in-house, or re-engineered, is a cross life cycle product that uses the design concepts and methodologies to generate user documentation, training scenarios, programming specifications, and conversion planning specifications. Therefore, it is a design document created equally by the information services personnel, the management team, and the end-users. The design, as modified by joint participation of all parties listed previously, actually bridges the communications gap between users and the technical staff, eliminating the problems that result from excluding users after their initial input. All subsequent tasks in the Cycle will be user defined and emanate directly from the design. Figure 1.2 illustrates the point. The design dictionary is the basis for the design. It guides the development phase, and it becomes the end-user documentation and training. As the design changes, the documentation and training change automatically.

THE COBRE GROUP

For the past five years, the COBRE Group, Inc., in Morristown, New Jersey, has developed generic templates of major applications for large software developers. The templates represent years of the software developer's experience with numerous systems. Using the latest Windows graphics and personal computer (PC) technology, and porting to UNIX, it had all major platforms. The design is in the following five levels of detail:

• System level, including clusters of like processes
• Decomposition of functions into more detailed components and modules
• Functionality level, including the primary system processes and data flows
• Procedural level (work statements), including detailed activities required for day-to-day operations of the system
• Screen format level, including formats, data elements, purpose, and edits (Forms and reports are also captured at this level.)

Underlying this structured methodology is a format of both processes and procedures that can be supported by data model formats (i.e., data-flow diagrams needed for structural analysis and leveling of the new system). If information services use CASE, Ways of Working accommodates CASE technology, but does not dictate and necessitate CASE.

This information, compiled logically with PC-based graphics technology, is the basis of the concept. From this, users can review the proposed system by the following:

• Business process and in the context of their daily operations.
• Procedure.
• Screen, data element, report, and form.
• Job description and organization.

At the same time, information services can review systems by the following:

• Index search.
• Data flow.
• Logical design down to the screen level.
• Requirements definition.

FIGURE 1.2
Cross Cycle Methodology

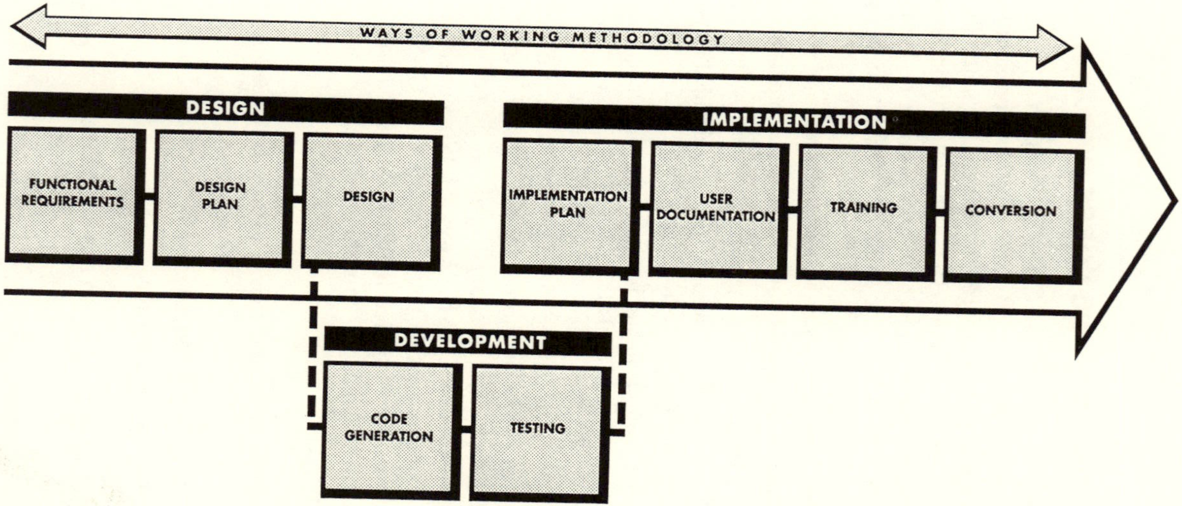

Information services personnel can then complete the programming and conversion tasks based on the agreed-to design. Project management can monitor the project while planning the cut-over with all hands on board. Training and user documentation are natural byproducts, not after-the-fact assignments for those not involved in the design in the first place.

ADDRESSING THE CYCLE AND APPLICATIONS SOFTWARE SHORTCOMINGS

This concept, as a cross life cycle product, can make any implementation strategy effective and workable. It attacks the major concerns in application development—time, costs, and risk. It is the design component and the focus for subsequent tasks in the Cycle. It reduces the time required for each step in the process, and therefore, the cost. It is based on five years of template development and leads to programming from the design, thus reducing the risk.

The concept directly enhances purchased software packages. COBRE has worked closely with several developers, including Ross Systems in Atlanta, Georgia, that uses it to assist its customers to do the following:

- It allows Ross users to understand the generic design and how it can meet their specific requirements.
- The users can modify their internal systems to meet changing conditions without risking loss of support or falling "out of phase" with the vendor.
- Ongoing joint application development assures that all interested parties will know the system, having been involved in adjusting to and understanding the design.
- It includes all implementation tools, such as plans, documentation, training, and conversion specifications.

Ross calls it SAM, meaning a full-strength implementation tool for its Fortune 1000 customer base.

Defining the Ways of Working opens up the potential for new application development within a realistic development life cycle without the long lead times, excessive costs, and unacceptable risks. This is because the design generates user documentation and training in exactly the same manner as for predefined software at Ross. SAM truly complements Ross software, according to management and users alike.

This framework for communication allows users to work independently on their needs, brainstorming new business and service ideas, while they look at diagrams on a display screen. The business users follow the systematic methodology available with graphics (much like CASE, except understandable to nontechnologists) and preserve a record of their ideas that can be analyzed later by information services. The software allows users to review and change diagrams of their business operation on the display screen for information services professionals who review their work later. The final system will not require voluminous manuals which are never read anyway. This will be discussed more later.

PROBLEM IDENTIFICATION

More sophisticated automated aid, based on the use of analytical and graphic software with the diagramming tools, can point out problems in proposed data usage or transaction handling that need resolution or investigation by the information services group or a consultant. The design eventually becomes the user documentation and training. This new framework of communication requires some support to users from information services, as they define current and future processes, although the business process users are able to specify in a more independent manner and design what they want a business application to do. This is the very basis of both re-engineering and systems integration. In both, it is imperative that we understand where we are, how we do things, and how business processes work.

REITERATIVE THINKING

Our definition of the Ways of Working provides business users more opportunity to shape how computers will be used. This, we believe, is the essential ingredient to success. One of the very real factors that has brought about this potential for change has been the increasing use of PCs by business users and the iterative processing mode of operation available with PCs. Administrators, business planners, accounting managers, and a host of others can learn to use sophisticated graphics and documentation tools on their personal computers or work stations to identify problems and re-engineer processes. Whether they are exploring an existing business process or building a new process, they go through an iterative process that involves starting with an idea of their initial needs, exploring alternatives, finding out how to set up or use computing to meet the initial set of needs, tailoring the solution to meet their needs more fully, and implementing the system in their environment for use by themselves or others. Users who engage in this iterative approach will find this approach to system development allows them to work independently on their business needs and then make use of tools and consultants that can guide them to a solution.

The iterative process is fundamental to successful design, re-engineering studies, systems integration projects, and the improvement of business processes. The concept involves communication of ideas between management users and information services.

NEED FOR A METHODOLOGY

Processes should not be redesigned without a structured methodology, but must not be shackled to the tired and old systems life cycle approach. In most cases, there is a desire to just do something and not worry about methodology. However, just as these business users often seek guidance on corporate objectives from management, they must work closely with the information services organization for aid in obtaining data from corporate databases, understanding communications facilities or new technical capabilities, and ultimately, re-engineering business processes.

We conducted a survey of large and small information services departments and a random sample of software developers. One clear finding was that users want to and should work closely with the information services departments in developing solutions to their informational problems. For example,

Support Desired by Users Engaged in Independent Systems Activities

Type of Problem	Support Desired from Information Services
Corporate data needed	Knowledge of databases and data communications links from local Personal Computers to the Mainframe
Aggregation of data	Means of converting and loading data in spreadsheets or Personal Computer databases
Communication with other departments	Network linkages (LAN and WAN requests) should be understood
Integrating applications	Means of reviewing results of integration

Source: The COBRE Group, Morristown, New Jersey.

Based on these findings, flexibility was incorporated into the Ways of Working concept. Access to data, networking, and use of PC-based tools are inherent in the concept today.

In this survey, we found some other interesting things about how companies are addressing the need for business processing and what they thought of classic CASE tools for the re-engineering process. These findings prompted the development of the Ways of Working concept to help users make a positive contribution to the re-engineering process. Our survey disclosed the following conclusions:

1. *CASE tools are not re-engineering tools.* CASE tools are for information services technicians to define structure and code systems. They cannot be justified on the basis of coding productivity improvements alone. The justification must span a larger portion of the life cycle to include maintenance, personnel turnover issues, upgrades, incorporating better designs, and so forth. Early proponents of CASE tools set a bad precedent by focusing on code productivity. Now the finance managers are perplexed by the absence of productivity gains and the high cost of CASE tool implementation.

2. *The greatest single impediment* for the acceptance of CASE tools is lack of vision on the part of information services and end-user management on how best to use them. Other reasons also cited are the following:

- The learning curve is too steep.
- The high cost of CASE tools.
- There is usually more functionality in it than you need to re-engineer.
- Dual level objections: For the programmers, it is job security; for management, it is the inability to cope with change. Taken together, they spell inaction.
- CASE is revolutionary, not evolutionary like most software and software developers are.
- Political environment.

3. *Misuse of CASE tools has bred contempt for all tools*:
   - Using CASE tools with a weak systems design or bad methodology only makes matters worse.
   - Using CASE tools without knowledgeable and committed end-user involvement causes misfires.
   - If you view CASE tools through your procedural past, then you will develop software with the same mistakes.
   - CASE is a catch-all phrase that is losing its meaning.
   - CASE is equated with risk.

4. *Very large users* with unique applications or databases are not good candidates for CASE tools. Beware!

5. *There is need for a good reliable, historical reference* and database of experiences for comparison purposes. Once that has been established, rational justification can take place.

6. *You do not have to resort to a CASE tool to improve a productivity.* You may use classic software development methods, but with a strict adherence to a methodology.

7. One problem with CASE tool acceptance is that it is viewed as a *product instead of a method.*

Some obvious conclusions are possible from this survey, and these conclusions were important in the design and implementation of the Ways of Working concept and where CASE tools should fit into the overall concept. We, the surveyors, have drawn the following five conclusions from this COBRE survey:

1. CASE tools were conceived for information services to cut development time, coding, and cost, and to improve quality.

2. CASE tools and users are oil and water.

3. CASE tools have had a negative impact on tools in general.

4. Tools, including CASE, require some vision.

5. CASE is not a viable tool for re-engineering business processes.

CASE tools have a valuable place in the world of information services, but do not address the need to rethink processes nor to enhance communications between technicians and systems users.

Our survey showed major dissatisfaction with the tools available to help users and information services technicians to design, redesign, and re-engineer business processes. The issue to us is simply one of communications and the need to understand our Ways of Working. Information services cannot communicate with users using entity-relation tables and data-flow diagrams. A major void existed and needed to be filled. However, we could see that entity-relation tables and data-flow diagrams could have substantial impact on information services and the final design.

Consequently, we reviewed the *capability* to incorporate data-flow diagrams (DFD) and entity-relation diagrams (ERD) into the design concept. We tied them to the user process flows, but incorporated the same hierarchy of design and presentation. Ways of Working can easily tie users to information services technicians to the benefit of all.

We asked, in our survey, if the company were involved in re-engineering. As we reported earlier, a vast majority is involved. We then asked the following three questions:

1. What tools are you prepared to use (or what is available to you)?
2. What do you think of CASE tools as re-engineering tools, and what has been your experience with CASE?
3. What tools, concepts (including templates), and graphic presentation software would be useful in re-engineering, design, and redesign of systems and processes?

We found the following:

1. The respondents were outspoken in their commitment to use whatever tools were available. They felt, however, that few tools actually existed. What existed and had been acquired lay unused with the label "shelfware."
2. CASE tools were not considered good re-engineering tools. Flow charts of processes were the most frequently mentioned method for re-engineering, but data-flow diagrams were never mentioned.
3. Exclusively, users cited word processing as a tool to write procedures. Some respondents used basic flow chart tools, but more sophisticated graphics were not mentioned, nor was the concept of hierarchy of design and presentation.

Our conclusion: A void exists in the knowledge of what is available, what can be used, and how a methodology could be helpful.

RESTRUCTURING INFORMATION SERVICES ROLES

What may come of all this may be the restructure of the role of information services into that of a consultant, rather than the organization solely responsible for application development. As a result of this restructuring, some information services organizations should set up rules or procedures for users to follow when they are going to participate in design and re-engineering projects. These procedures may involve the use of an information center or an environment developed specifically for user-developed systems. An effort has usually been made in these procedures to have larger systems developed under the direction of the information services group and with an established methodology of planning, documentation, and data tracking.

It may be true that there are some approaches to system redesign that are different from the methodologies utilized by the information services organizations. Application systems developed by users or information services vendors with new approaches to project methodology are more visible in the PC area, but they can be encountered in the use of larger computers as well. They resulted from actions by users who were frustrated over requirements that were misunderstood by the information services group and delays in having new business capabilities introduced that required systems changes.

If end-users take on the development of systems and re-engineering of business processes, they may need to try new methodologies as well as new tools. However, users are limited in their awareness and use of most tools except word processes and spreadsheets to solve problems. For example, we found

Software Technology Mentioned	Frequency of Mention
Spreadsheets	High
Relational databases	Some use of PC-based development tools
Fourth-generation languages	Few
Proto-typing	Some, but few
Automated analysis/design	Information services only
Code generation	Very low including information services
Graphical analysis aids/multimedia	Low
AI/expert systems	Very low
Computer-based training	Low

Users are not using what is available to them, even if they are getting involved with information services and trying to contribute to the design process. It seems to be an individual thing. There is no concentrated effort to use readily available systems, tools, and concepts.

USE OF METHODOLOGIES

Although few users employ tools, some business users have shown a propensity to dispense with the time and effort of using a formal methodology in favor of a more iterative approach to application design. As one user at a large manufacturer stated, "If we can generate or find application software that is possible to test, train the staff for and install in our environment, we want to try using it." Nevertheless, some users are willing to consider corporate-wide data communication and information resource guidelines in solving business problems, and believe that hardware, software, and data management restrictions should not limit the ability of users to design solutions to problems more quickly or with less cost.

MORE USER INVOLVEMENT

The change we are promoting is a movement away from complex methodological CASE tools that emphasize (1) the role of systems professionals, and (2) the process of review and sign off by users of something they do not understand to a new atmosphere of greater and more creative user involvement in system development and re-engineering. A new approach that focuses on graphical depictions of business processes should emerge as a result of increased user involvement, and it offers considerable promise to business because it allows business users to become more active and creative in defining problems, generating solutions, and re-engineering business processes. Information services management and far-sighted industry leaders must emphasize the need for user involvement now and publicize the problems arising when it is not practiced.

This new approach is encouraging people involved in problems to move away from bureaucratic approaches for reaching a solution that bears no relation to the situation. They must seek problem-solving approaches that allow them to make more use of their own and other user's knowledge about the factors involved. This is very consistent with Hammer's proposition that we should "nuke" those processes and start over with consensus and involvement. That is what the Japanese have taught us.

In order to progress along these lines, the information services staffs that are involved have to rethink their own participation, the participation and roles of support personnel or other groups, and the framework of communication that is being used to describe, analyze, and develop solutions to problems and the re-engineering of processes. This framework has to be a freeway for communicating ideas about problems and possible solutions, rather than machinery for grinding out a solution whether the users who are involved can fully understand the process or support the solution. It is a new look at our Ways of Working, documented with a proven methodology supported by current technology.

2

Feasible Involvement: A New Joint Application Development Scheme?

The process of improving operations is a joint venture with the users involved. It is not a revolutionary concept, but the truth is, it has been difficult for business process users to get on board with the fast-changing technology under the direction of information services. It would be an advantage if we could do so.

The idea of having people who are involved with problems review the situation by themselves is a good one. They can apply their knowledge and the knowledge of experts in the field at the same time the ideas they have formulated are being communicated to specialists in the information services department. To address business problems and opportunities, users and management should be able to think and review their own needs, existing systems, and accumulated industry experience in what appears to them to be a completely unfettered environment. These participants include the clerks and supervisors who pass on their ideas about what should be done (the design of the new business system) for later technical analysis by information services professionals. Participation by intelligent and articulate information services staff members without user involvement and at too early a stage can introduce ideas about solutions before a business problem is completely reviewed, relevant industry experience and developments have been analyzed, or business personnel have thought about the business processes that seem desirable from their perspective.

In order for business users to have an effective method of independently reviewing business problems or needs, a means of visually walking through existing manual and automated systems is needed so users do not have to rely on information services personnel to explain how systems function. A number of approaches for accomplishing this have now been implemented on personal computers, including the approach called *Ways of Working*. The process of visually reviewing and analyzing business application systems and the effect of new ideas on a display screen can also provide a means of recording the ideas users develop so they can be analyzed by the information services group and fed back to the users for possible changes (i.e., the iterative process). The ideas and system changes should be captured in a systematic methodology using graphics products. This really is the concept of joint application development but with a new twist. We believe that joint application development (JAD) and rapid application development (RAD) have not caught on for several important reasons. First, in reading about these techniques and in conversations with IBM and other practitioners, we have concluded that the JAD and RAD processes are rigid and formalized to a fault. According to our sources, clear and unfettered interchange of ideas is seldom achieved. The reason is obvious; users and information services technicians come from different backgrounds, approach problem solving and systems design and re-engineering from a different perspective, and speak different languages.

A second complication to effective JAD/RAD is the "Tabula Rasa" syndrome. That is the ineffective approach of gathering a group of users and developers in a room and starting the session with a blank piece of paper. So how do we process an order in our current system? Silence prevails. The alternative is to have developed a model or prototype of the way things are and begin discussions from this point.

A third complication is the inexplicable determination to define systems and business processes using the epitome of noncommunications between users and technicians, that is, the CASE tool with its data-flow diagrams, entity-relations tables, and data breakdown charts. IBM, in a presentation on JAD in Los Angeles a few years ago, described their JAD strategy as follows: The users and designers meet in the front of the room. They proceed, during the day-long session, to describe and define a new or "to be re-engineered" system. In the back of the room, there sits an information services technician with paper and pad on his or her lap, taking notes on the proceedings. The notes are converted to data-flow diagrams that are presented to users the next day. Our conclusion is that this is not a good approach, as users do not relate to CASE methodologies that were not designed for them in the first place. They do not understand data-flow diagrams.

WALL CHARTS

Then there is the wall-charts approach used by many, including one of the largest system integrators in this country. I sat astounded when a reasonably astute vice president of this consulting firm tried to rationalize wall charts.

His point was that every employee in the organization wants to see how he or she fits into the process. In addition, he struggled, they like to see what contribution they have made by seeing their own handwriting or "mark." The concept may be true, but the methodology is wrong. We urge participation, but not with brown wrapping paper. The wall chart, of course, is a flow chart of the business processes spread around the room like a shroud. The idea, incredibly, is that you flow chart the existing process on the first shroud. Then you remove that one and flow chart the improved, re-engineered process on another one, putting it on the wall. Or you may put stick-ums on it to show areas of potential improvement. Consistently, practitioners of wall charting admit the difficulty of comparing the proposed (now on the wall) with the existing (now in the trash basket).

The wall chart, with the obvious deficiency identified previously, has other major deficiencies. This method of defining and re-engineering process does not

1. Take advantage of existing technologies such as graphics, screen design and capture, or analysis tools including the common spreadsheet.
2. Allow analysis of both process flows and data flows in a comprehensible way.
3. Utilize the concept of iteration.
4. Benefit from the mind soothing and clear comprehension that results from decomposition of systems to processes and subsequently to work statements (procedures).

So if this large consulting firm recommends wall charting, you should politely say no, thank you. This is a marvelous way to weed out the numerous consulting firms that will want to re-engineer your company. We replaced this firm with a client in Europe by simply quantifying our procedures and processes. The consulting firm proposed doing this manually with a calculator. We programmed it to quantify our processes and eliminated a costly consultant.

Changes to designs and recommended re-engineering projects can be controlled internally using tools, a methodology, and software that will facilitate the review of processes in a mode understood by all. That would allow users and management to feel completely comfortable when calling on their own and industry experience and knowledge to plan changes and define new systems approaches. Users, themselves, reviewing user business application planning, can take advantage of available graphics software to guide planning or raise questions about proposed data usage or processing. An outline of this approach is seen in Figure 2.1.

The critical design concept is the Business Knowledge Repository, which contains flow charts of all business processes in one Ways of Working directory. The flow of business process incorporates any or all of the following:

I. *Inputs*
   1. User-defined system requirements to make sure that the process satisfies the business needs.

FIGURE 2.1
Facilitate the Review Process

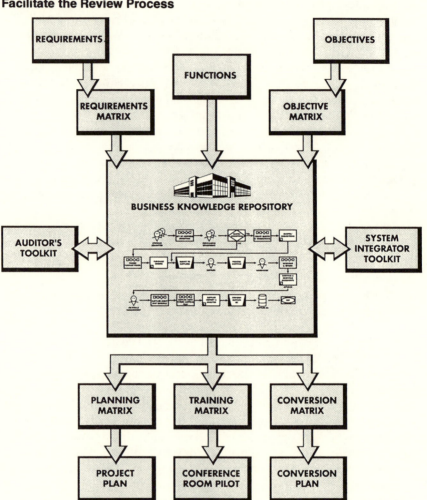

2. Functions to assure completeness of design and process.

3. Objectives to make sure the design addresses the goals for new or modified systems (e.g., reduce inventory, improve order processing cycle, etc.).

II. *Outputs*

1. Planning considerations as a base for design development and implementation (the Systems Development Life Cycle).

2. Training components leading to training scenarios, and ultimately, a conference room pilot capability.

3. Data for data conversion.

III. *Involvement*

    1. Auditor's tool kit for auditing the process would include clear flows, procedures, audit points, and rules.

    2. System integrator kit to identify use of hardware and software.

This approach to re-engineering business processes and subsequent new or modified business application development is timely and "on target."

Having more user involvement in the Ways of Working provides the opportunity for the information services group to devote itself more to technology-intensive activities, such as developing and managing corporate networks and information assets, as well as to invest time in new types of capabilities to support an increase of productivity in user-development environments. It may be referred to as managing the complexity. It will also reduce or eliminate the presence of information services in the types of development activities that now result in problems; for example, information services developing systems without a thorough knowledge of the application environment.

This approach further provides a more meaningful role for the outside consultant to review current practices. This is their strength because they have "seen it all before" in other similar situations. The best firms should have databases of processes' typical bottlenecks and successful solutions. This objective view is good and recommended.

HIGH INTEREST

Process improvement is of high current interest because of the pressure for new system capabilities to meet critical business needs, such as cost reduction or the introduction of new products and services. Many companies are continually frustrated by failures and delays in plans to develop and keep computer applications responsive to the needs of business users. There is a growing feeling that computer applications have to be easier to generate and modify, as well as easier for users to understand and integrate into their business activities. This has been a perplexing problem in the past.

At present, the development of complex new business computing systems and additions to old ones, as well as the use of new technical capabilities, results in a stream of additions to the backlog queue, the list of changes and enhancements to application systems requested by users and management. Some development activities also require major changes after they have been started, and some are scrapped. There is a general feeling in companies encountering these problems that information services management and the methods they are utilizing for development have not kept pace with the development of technology.

We observed in Chapter 1 that reactions to these problems have included: outsourcing; restructuring the information services function; experimenting with new development capabilities, such as CASE; and using information services vendors, who supposedly have appropriate industry experience together with technical capabilities for systems integration; and redesigning processes. However, what is really needed in addition to or in support of these changes is to improve the ability of users and corporate management to plan and review what they want and to adequately understand and control what is being developed. What is needed is a better way to look at our business processes through the definition of Ways of Working and through the use of existing technologies. Software exists that provides an easily understood record of what proposed business systems are supposed to do. Software exists that helps to control and monitor projects. A methodology exists that can make it possible for business users to easily compare what they want with the system that is being implemented. The time is right for changes in current approaches and methodologies in the development of business applications. The Ways of Working approach will allow corporations to speed up and better control the development process since user review of requirements and proposed systems can be handled more rapidly. Users will use this method to describe their requirements or what a new system should accomplish. What is holding up the process?

WHAT MUST BE OVERCOME

The two primary reasons that it may be difficult for corporations to reconsider the use of new techniques to aid users, information services, and management in systems development are (1) the rapidly increasing availability of new tools, techniques, and capabilities being utilized, and (2) the current complexity of business applications that are being developed. It is difficult, particularly for information services, to devote attention to all new approaches when it appears that considerable effort is needed to understand and manage the development of existing business systems whether a new approach might eventually simplify the process. This is a major reason why CASE tools are not used more often; information services now perceives them as slowing the process, not reducing development time. The long learning curve and the time required to develop the design itself are problems. Managers do not, according to our survey, take the longer-term view that "better design means better systems," and thus, less long-term maintenance. The demand for quicker reaction to market demands for information are counter to the design dictates of CASE tools. In addition, the demand for more information in a more timely fashion has added complexity to current applications requiring a much better understanding of how things work.

This illustrates the difficulty of incorporating new ideas or changes. A problem is the inadequacy of current development approaches and methodologies, and the lack of communication between users and the information services staff that these methodologies foster. What is recommended here is a new approach that can produce immediate results in most cases by providing users a means of more easily reviewing what the new application will be doing.

The new approach is user-friendly, so to speak; users can train themselves and their staffs. More intense involvement of users in application planning and review can result and provide important benefits:

- Business applications can be re-engineered more efficiently rather than just automated.
- Users, as well as information services personnel, will be used productively on application development work and design.
- The challenge of obtaining complete and accurate requirements can be moved forward to the users' domain.
- Decisions on what to develop immediately or add later with modifications can be made jointly and more intelligently.
- Training and documentation become natural byproducts, not neglected afterthoughts.

USE OF GRAPHICS

A new approach for re-engineering, systems development, and implementation that incorporates visual techniques to assist user participation would not only speed up the process of obtaining solutions to business problems, but also address the issue of obtaining complete and accurate systems requirements. Many failures to fully meet application requirements, as well as continual requests to change and modify systems which add to backlogs in system development, could be avoided or reduced by using a new concept in system development that utilizes graphical displays of business systems together with an organized change in approach toward application development and the old bug-a-boo, the vaunted system development life cycle. New multimedia and graphics now are not used effectively. This visual concept, which could shorten the system-development life cycle for new systems in most cases, requires changes in the relationship and framework of communication between information services departments, users, and management. It would lead to a new and more cost-effective way to use outside consultants as well. It does not focus merely on improving the ability of users to participate in systems activities. It reorients system activities to business processes so they will respond to the functional needs of users and corporate management and incorporate the knowledge of business users. The framework for communication of business development plans and needs between users, management, and information services is a visual, graphic description of business processes that users can easily understand and modify to describe requirements or our Ways of Working. This enables those with business knowledge and those who plan to have more of an impact on system planning. Using systems templates and flow charts, users can design or review business processes or our Ways of Working as they did in the earlier days of information processing—even before the use of computers.

A new methodology—Ways of Working—is available and has been used to improve project planning, documentation, training, conversion, and acceptance testing by providing diagrams or pictures that review exactly what is being done in relation to a project in a form that business users and others can easily review. It can make reality out of the desire to improve business processes. It can make re-engineering projects doable, and equally as important, make cost justifiable with one big boost to the opportunity for success in streamlining the enterprise.

Process improvements can be expedited by new methodologies supported by software technology. To take advantage of these, however, it is necessary to change existing applications to use the new technology. Change does not come easily; it is an obstacle. Demands for the development of new application systems that advances in technology may have just made possible might also lead to application backlogs. For example, advances in online and storage technology and the use of Windows, graphical user interfaces, and hypertext add to the demand for new application systems—and probably new backlogs exacerbating the information services problem.

Backlogs can result from changes that are necessary to meet new government regulations or changes in organization or products. In addition, backlogs can include plans to rebuild entire systems or major portions of systems that do not perform the job they were designed for because business methods or markets have changed or business operations were not understood well enough. These types of backlogs can be understood by users, even if they add to the delays in implementing work. Requests to modify old or even new systems to correct problems that resulted from misinterpreted or misunderstood requirements are hard to tolerate. As research indicates, misunderstood requirements are a major contributor to the need to correct or rebuild systems and to re-engineer business processes.

Where misunderstood or incomplete, requirements have had an impact on the backlog queue. Business users must become more involved in systems activities and the search for new methods and tools to more accurately describe needs and more rapidly develop systems. The collection of methods and tools that can be used for this purpose are described as the definitive Ways of Working.

CONCLUSION

Current methods provide the opportunity for users to more easily review requirements, re-engineer processes, and design the business system applications that will satisfy them. It also enables the information services group to become more involved in business application planning processes with the user at a much higher level than programming specifications. The information services staff will not be required to interpret written documentation for applications. As a result of these improvements in communication, business users will have more assurance that the requirements they are describing will be implemented.

In addition, current methodologies permit the specifications and design for system changes or new developments that users have developed to be employed in automating or aiding development, as well as in aiding project planning, training, and conversion. Current methods can also be used to introduce or convert to new hardware, take advantage of systems integration, and state-of-the-art software technology by providing a diagram of the steps that are planned, which can be updated or changed over time. These benefits are produced by extending the use of software technology to track the process (the manual and automated steps) or our Ways of Working—and to track that process graphically rather than by tedious narrative.

The result is a new involvement in re-engineering and application development, and in the use of graphics by users who are increasingly more computer literate from training in high school and college. In addition to using word processing and spreadsheets to automate their less complex information requirements, users are able to define what they need as the information services staff works on complex communications problems while reducing the backlog of demands. We believe that these factors, increasing computer literacy, overburdened information services staffs, and the availability of new graphical tools will lead users to a new stage of involvement, where they will participate in or produce larger, more complex, mission-critical systems. What is needed now is simply to understand this new framework or methodology, and we will improve the ability of users to understand and control what is being developed. The tools and methods, the Ways of Working, designed for users to impact re-engineering projects and define application systems, are available today.

The following can be accomplished:

- Users can review the functions of application software packages from vendors by following graphical diagrams. Modifications that are desired can be indicated by making changes to the diagrams on the screen.

- Users can define what they want an application to do by reviewing a basic version or template of the application in a graphical diagram on a display screen. The template diagrams can be modified by the user to indicate unique requirements.

- Changes that are made to diagrams of applications on a screen or new diagrams of applications that are drawn by users can be reviewed by information services staff. They can provide advice or guidance to users on the flow of data, the use of data resources, and other development considerations without intruding on business planning.

You may call it business modeling, but it is not the esoteric methodologies understood only by trained information services professionals. It is a user tool and methodology which we call the Ways of Working.

A Case in Point

Sometimes, we do not get good advice. A case in point concerns a large West Coast utility who rightfully selected Ross's manufacturing system.

Ross had adopted the Ways of Working concept to define its excellent client–server manufacturing software system. The resulting product—a true implementation tool kit—is named SAM. SAM incorporates a detailed implementation plan, multilevel business process and work statement templates, and data setup and mapping into a single system, operating our ten plus platforms in a local area network environment. Today, SAM is offered to users of the Ross system. It was designed to replace user manuals, although customers can opt for the written word if they so desire. Most do not.

Almost all new users of Ross, after viewing SAM, choose it as the implementation toolset. The utility's steering committee reviewed SAM and liked what it saw. No less than three committee members, including the chairperson, approved the concept and recommended adaptation of this strategy for its implementation effort.

As part of the implementation process, the utility hired a large consulting firm. This firm also reviewed SAM, and in lip-service only, praised it. The senior partner endorsed it openly. The younger consultants, straight from B-schools, openly recommended SAM as the best way to define procedures and document processes. But a strange thing occurred. Senior management side-tracked the acquisition for weeks, telling me and Ross that organizational issues were taking priority. Week after week we called to find out when SAM should be delivered. Not now, we heard, even though all of the approvals were in place. As the reader may surmise, it was all a ruse. Behind the scenes, and with a naïve misinformed project manager in the dark, the consulting firm's senior members completely re-wrote every procedure in Word. Nothing wrong with Word, but this was very expensive and an inadequate duplication. The new Word procedures did not differ at all from SAM because the utility in question was implementing the software without modification.

The consultant here was dishonest: first, in stringing the software vendor along; second, in charging the customer for unnecessary work; and third, for developing a product with none of the capabilities of the implementation tool, SAM. These procedures will not be read, they will never be maintained, and they will never afford the ability to view Ways of Working for any number of different perspectives.

We can only conclude that the drive for billable hours, in this instance, outweighed the customer's best interests. Beware.

3

The Search for Tools,
Methods, and Involvement

Ways of Working is a methodology wrapped in a tool. The concept or methodology is patented (Patent 5,321,610, June 14, 1994, U.S. Patent Office). We like to refer to it as the common sense approach that can be used and understood by management, end-users, and information services professionals. It grew out of a real need and was created to improve communications between users and technicians. It was also created to increase the efficiency of consultants, allowing them to consult rather than define current systems that the client knows better than they do. It grew out of a need for usable tools for users. It makes it possible to document our Ways of Working only once, then to view it from different perspectives, such as actively based costing, quality assurance, and disaster planning.

A LITTLE ON TOOLS

The introduction of tools oriented to information services professionals and their development activities started with the use of timesharing. Timesharing not only brought the use of computing to the desktop, it also encouraged the introduction of software applications that had user-friendly features and interactive development tools, such as TSO (timesharing option) on mainframes that had a significant effect on productivity.

A succession of interactive tools and workbenches have followed TSO, and together with academic and industry research on productivity, led to the development of software engineering tools and methodologies for the information services staff. Other developments that led to software engineering included the use of tools to draw flow charts from existing software in the 1960s and the use of decision tables and other methods of stating requirements that could be used to generate software in the 1960s and 1970s.

SOFTWARE ENGINEERING

A surge of growth in software engineering started in the late 1970s with the introduction of structured methods that allowed the information services organization to document requirements and the design of applications in a much more organized and consistent manner. Software tools followed in the 1980s that allowed structured methods to be employed so a display screen on a mainframe terminal or on a PC would provide visual diagrams of data flows, called data-flow diagrams, and data element relationships in existing or proposed applications. From these, data definitions and even coding could be generated. In addition to these tools, code generators that work from a simplified language and reverse engineering software tools that make use of existing coding have been introduced in the 1980s. For example:

- Automated analysis and design packages such as Knowledgeware and IEF that run on mainframes and personal computers.
- Analysis and design products, such as IEF (Texas Instruments), for personal computers that will help to generate codes.
- Code generators such as Telon that interface to analysis and design tools (a total set of capabilities such as Pacbase of CGI that has analysis and design tools, a 4GL, program generator, and a database capability).
- Reverse engineering tools such as the Bachman products that help rebuild databases or applications.

These, however, are all information services tools which are incomprehensible to end-users and nontechnicians.

The introduction of CASE tools has been promoted by some information services departments, since they offer the possibility of speeding up development and provide information services with tools to document requirements that are complete and consistent. Visual displays of existing and proposed systems are easier for information services personnel to review than printed documentation. They are also available with some popular CASE packages and are front-end tools. These techniques have been successfully used by information services technicians, but remain remote from the user community.

The limited use of the user review and sign-off function in the life-cycle project methodology during the 1970s helped to focus more attention on the need for an improved user role in system development to solve the problem of checking that requirements were fully and adequately defined. A number of users stated during this period, if asked and included in the process, that they were signing off on requirements only to the extent that they could follow and understand them. The level of understanding was (and still is) very low.

Systems professionals must recognize that users face a difficult challenge in reviewing a written functional description of their requirements, since they are stated in a manner that tries to eliminate redundancy but repeats many words and ideas in an attempt to be logically complete and coherent. Past surveys have found that users feel the wording in requirements documentation can be compared to the contents of government or legal publications.

Adequate visual methods for reviewing applications or developing and analyzing requirements for new systems are needed to make more use of the experience and knowledge of business users and management. This knowledge cannot be taken advantage of unless the users are provided with tools that allow them not just to understand what an application does, but to follow and experiment with the flow of the application. These tools can allow users to investigate and design business systems that will meet competition and improve methods of doing business.

The tools can also allow business users to review application packages used by competitors or other companies that might provide an opportunity to improve revenues or save costs. This is true if the vendor provides such tools. Computer Associates in Islandia, New York, is one such vendor; Ross Systems in Atlanta, Georgia, is another. Ross Systems has all but perfected the approach.

If users and management were given the chance to review application packages available from vendors through these new visual methods, they might consider tradeoffs in system or business activities to implement the software package. If these techniques reveal that available software cannot be easily used or modified to meet their needs, business users might still have gained knowledge that would help them to plan a new application. A business user who had an opportunity to employ one of these methods stated that it was the most effective lesson in computer literacy he had ever experienced.

We can see all of this now by reviewing two current approaches to improving business processes: system integration and re-engineering. In each, we will discuss the need for user involvement, tools, and methodologies.

TOOLS FOR SYSTEMS INTEGRATION

One method of reviewing and possibly using the experience available in the industry has grown rapidly during the 1980s. This method, systems integration, involves the use of a vendor as a prime or lead contractor to select appropriate hardware and software—with modifications if necessary—to meet the needs of an organization.

This method has been used by companies to find and modify application solutions used elsewhere, as well as to have new technology and techniques

incorporated into application solutions. System integration is most successful when the entire existing system is reviewed by users and internal information services or an information services vendor.

Systems integration not only succeeds in using industry knowledge available outside a company, it makes more use of the business knowledge in a
company by giving users and management a more active role in reviewing
and selecting applications and in planning modifications to them, as will be
illustrated.

Opportunity for User Review

- Vendors conduct a more intensive review of user needs than is conducted in-house
  by traditional methods.
- Proponents normally are aware of new developments in the industry and review
  them with users.
- Applications at other companies are reviewed with users to uncover applicable ideas.
- The project uncovers ideas of users about support, functions, communications, and
  interfaces.

Systems integration requires new means of communication between information services personnel and users and corporate management to more fully
utilize the knowledge and experience in a company and review developments
in the industry that could be of interest. System integrators have also provided the means for clients to learn about and introduce new technology.
They have been particularly active in introducing new development techniques
and products that can ensure user needs are met and improve the development process. Systems integration supplies a model of the framework of communication that the information services group needs in work with users. But
system integration will only succeed if the prime vendor can communicate
effectively with users and management about needs, current applications, and
possible integration of systems or databases.

RE-ENGINEERING

Michael Hammer either coined this term, made it popular, or both. It makes
sense in that business may be considered a series of functions or processes.
They are, for example, entering a customer order, checking customer credit,
sending the order to manufacturing or distribution, billing the customer, setting up an accounts receivable entry, and applying cash. Each of these is a
business process. How well we do these has a major impact on how we perform, profit, and compete.

Re-engineering is the process of analyzing these business processes and
changing them to maximize productivity, cutting the time required to perform them, infusing quality into the process, and simply making them better.

It has been observed that re-engineering may be viewed as the following three components:

1. *Redesign*, which is developing new ways to process transactions and to do business.
2. *Retooling*, which is to build whole new systems to support the enterprise.
3. *Reorchestrating*, which is to associate and integrate new processes and new systems into the entire enterprise.

These components indicate the totality of re-engineering. As discussed in the Preface, Hammer does not recommend minor tweaking, but rather "nuk[ing] them."

One of the most well-known cases of re-engineering is the study at Ford Motor Company. It occurred in the accounts payable department, which was made up of 500 clerks. Ford observed that a competitor, although smaller, had only five clerks, which was clearly out of proportion to the vast array Ford employed. To address this issue, Ford analyzed the process from requisition to purchase order to matching receivers and issuing payments. Minor tweaking produced minor improvements.

Ford, at that time, took a step back and observed that certain functions were essential, but an inordinate amount of time was spent on payments requiring no deviation from the vendor invoice. Ford instituted automatic payments under most conditions, thus saving significant time and costs. Another guru tells that the way to improve our competitive position is to cut the time required to complete a business process; that is, the time required to introduce a new product, to process a customer order, and to make a manufactured replacement part. All this is possible as a result of re-engineering studies, and in fact, reduction in time is a major objective of re-engineering studies.

Re-engineering and systems integration are processes and studies. The first step in both is to analyze the present situation and document how things are being done with our Ways of Working. This, we contend, is a combined responsibility of management, the end-user, and the information services professional. Yet we have observed that communication between the three is less than perfect.

Re-engineering studies are, more often than not, contracted out to large consulting organizations. The rationale, which might be questioned, is that the consulting firms may be more objective in their review, as opposed to an in-house study conducted by the people who designed and implemented the process systems in the first place. The other rationale, of course, is the consultant's experience in doing similar studies and the diverse knowledge and training they can bring to the study. What tools do they bring with them? In most cases, none.

Some firms may tout their knowledge and use of CASE tools. As has been discussed, we believe that CASE tools are not the best for describing existing processes. CASE tools are automated methodologies, such as data-flow, entity-relation, and action diagrams. CASE tools clearly have a role in the design of systems for information services professionals. They are not tools to promote communications between management, end-users, and information services professionals. So we advocate, if end-users and management are to be heavily involved and contribute to the solutions sought in re-engineering studies, the CASE tools are not the tools for these studies.

Some firms, on the other hand, offer no automated tools to assist in their analysis other than spreadsheets. Incredibly, we observed a prominent consulting arm of a Big Six accounting firm perform a one-year analysis of the customer service process—manually. Very highly paid senior consultants interviewed everybody in sight and manually flow charted and documented the process. You cannot possibly imagine the amount of paper generated in this study.

In another situation, we walked into the project room of a major manufacturer in Chapter 11. All four walls were covered with process flow charts in the most detail imaginable. We were informed that this illustrated the way they send an order to the plant. Next month they planned to take these flow charts down from the four walls and start flow charting how they would improve the process. There was no integration, no synergy, no way to model different approaches, no user involvement, and no way to avoid a terminal Chapter 11.

What is needed in re-engineering studies is a clear methodology backed with sophisticated tools to assist in the study. What is also needed is a determination by the customer or client to insist that the consultant (or in-house study team) have an approach supported by methods and tools. One should never retain a consultant or undertake a study without a proven methodology and fourth-generation technology.

A CALL FOR INVOLVEMENT

The increasing use of systems integration and re-engineering developments in software engineering and the development of applications on PCs all call for an increasing role of the user in application development. Users must increase their role in describing requirements and designing what an application should do in business terms. The graphic techniques that allow business users to describe or review requirements and new or existing applications can support this increasing role. They can provide an improved means for users to communicate with the information services organization, vendors, or software engineering systems used to automate development. These techniques can show how business requirements and ideas flow from business objectives without being affected by technical considerations. As IBM has noted in its recent statements on advanced application development, planning must start with business objectives and ideas.

Improvements to support user planning techniques for application system development are anticipated in a host of software engineering products, as well as in expert systems and object-oriented developments. Expert systems are being explored that can guide users in the development of functional systems with CASE analysis and design tools. The expert system would indicate the implications of functional plans in relation to the use of data resources, transaction processing, and other aspects of information systems and suggest design steps in accordance with business objectives that will stay within time and cost constraints. This software will offer steps beyond "help" functions in regard to planning the design of business systems.

Object-oriented techniques are being explored for the improvement of the display graphics used to present descriptions of application systems to users, as well as to record the changes they make to these descriptions which indicate their unique business requirements. Work has also taken place with object-oriented techniques that can provide users with the means of combining functions from various applications in different programming languages. This work could provide users with the capability to make substantial changes in business processing without being limited by the obstacle of installed application systems that would require years to upgrade.

Object-oriented techniques are also being used to support new means of relating information that respond to the need for graphical or visual means of planning and reviewing ideas, rather than voluminous printouts.

PROGRESS

Progress has been made over the past twenty years in the introduction of software tools to aid systems analysts and the information services function in the development of application systems. Examples include the following:

- Database systems
- Fourth-generation languages
- Sophisticated utilities
- Software engineering tools

Progress is also shown in the growth of package solutions—particularly in vertical markets—such as manufacturing, distribution, and banking; and in standard generic applications such as general ledger, accounts payable, accounts receivable, and payrolls. Project management software has also grown to become an important tool in supporting and controlling large complex projects. Spreadsheets, database systems, and word processing systems abound and are increasingly sophisticated. The introduction of the systems development life cycle put structure in the design and development process. The life cycle became supported by new structured techniques and was subsequently modified to reflect the use of these methods or techniques.

More recently, computer users have sought ways to streamline their development process and improve business processes. The advent of systems integration has aided them by making it possible to move away from dedicated vendors (hardware or software) to open systems and take advantage of the technologies of multiple vendors. Systems integration makes it possible to achieve an "open architecture." Re-engineering makes it possible to improve business processes.

But systems integration and all their benefits depend heavily on user involvement in both the review and design phases. Again, we are hit by the reality that technicians and users do not have the best means to communicate—one knows the technology and the other the application. So how can the re-engineers and the integrators succeed? They have succeeded in a number of situations by using the skills of people trained in industries and applications—as well as technology—who spend the time necessary to walk through problems, existing systems, and development tasks with users. Improved means are available now, however, to assist users to review their needs and existing systems and what is being developed without the intensive methods and costs of systems integration.

It is a fact that over 60 percent of re-engineering studies fail. This is because of lack of user involvement and avoiding the reality that new proposals and recommendations must be implemented. Too often, users are not involved and little consideration is given to how this change must come about. Too often, the critical importance of the current business process and the chaos associated with changing it are underestimated. It is unnecessary. Defining our Ways of Working at the procedural or work statement level and providing a means to view them from any number of perspectives is a workable concept. Management can view the entire order processing chain from order to manufacture to customer, in a logical format it understands. It begins, however, with the definition of our Ways of Working.

A NEW LEGITIMACY

Several firms exist that provide analysis of the trends in current business and information processing in particular. The Yankee Group in downtown Boston, Massachusetts, is one of them. The Yankee Group has recognized the need for implementation tools. It has recognized and reported on the emergence of a new set of tools, referred to as a new class of business engineering and implementation tools that combine modeling, best practices, simulation, configuration, and project management. Ways of Working is listed as one of these emerging tools. It has been given legitimacy, according to Yankee management, because one company, SAP, recognized the need.

4

Current State of Business Processes

The state of business processes is extremely turbulent at this time. We have spent an enormous amount of time and effort in developing new concepts and processes in manufacturing, but very little effort in dealing with administrative, marketing, and financial processes. In manufacturing we began with material requirements planning (MRP), which is the process of exploding customer demands into its component parts, and with the power of computers, developing ordering and manufacturing rules. We then expanded the process to MRP II, which is the original concept of MRP, but not integrated with the financial data generated in the enterprise.

Some processes have been studied in the manufacturing area; for example, much has been said about how the Japanese run their manufacturing operations. We analyzed KANBAN systems, which are a means of passing notes to indicate what items and what quantities of products are required at the work stations in sequence. We explored, evaluated, and implemented cell technologies, which were the manufacturing entities making products in the plant. We are now benefiting from the concept of just-in-time (JIT). JIT is the logical process of reducing work-in-process inventories and purchased parts inventories by identifying only that which we need and requisitioning it to arrive on the dock or be manufactured to arrive at the next station just-in-time.

It seems, however, that we have not given the same thought and analysis to business processes, such as processing a customer order. Not much seems to have changed in processing purchase requisitions and purchase orders. Accounting processes, such as applying cash, have not changed for decades. Warehousing also seems to have been overlooked to some extent.

In a time when we are becoming more service oriented and when we believe that customer satisfaction is critical to a successful enterprise, we have ignored many common business processes for a long time. The information services sector has been focused too, but not on business processes and their improvement. Information services has concentrated on software re-engineering. New software re-engineering products have been introduced that offer new levels of productivity in development of software applications, and they have grown at an extremely rapid rate during the past five years. Over 130 vendors are now offering software re-engineering products, so many that consolidation among the vendors has started to take place. It is interesting to notice, however, that this effort has not been well thought out. There are no consistent standards developed for these software engineering products, nor is there a general approach or two or three basic approaches for using these products together with other application tools and techniques, such as prototyping or fourth-generation languages. This lack of standards has an overall negative impact on re-engineering of software that should not deter the business processing re-engineering efforts.

Software re-engineering, of course, is the restructuring of those old CO-BOL programs. IBM, Data General, and DEC, as well as many software and professional service vendors, are now developing products and formulating application development strategies that will address the use of software re-engineering products, but major questions remain in the mind of some business users and information services managers. They believe they need techniques or products that provide an overall view of a business application from a business perspective, not just the COBOL code, which can also be used to supply information for process re-engineering and development. This is one of the needs we are addressing today; the areas of software and business re-engineering are desperate disciplines.

According to a recent study performed by the COBRE Group in Morristown, New Jersey, which we previously discussed, users have their concerns divided between (1) current problems involving business systems and processes that are unresponsive to their needs, (2) the use of software re-engineering or other development techniques that do not address their needs for new systems, (3) the potential for PCs with advanced tools, and (4) applications software to replace all these COBOL programs. Each of these revolves around users' concerns for current business processes.

A study of business processes implemented during the past three years clearly sets forth the concerns of users about the state of current processes. According to business groups that use the systems, approximately 40 percent of the systems developed need changes or upgrades, and almost one-third of the systems need major rebuilding. Some of the systems that need major rebuilding are of questionable use to the company. The business users are particularly concerned about the fact that it may be difficult and time consuming to upgrade these systems, that there were lengthy queues of work to be done on systems by the information services group, and that, therefore, help may not be in the offing.

Although it is not surprising to find out that changes are needed in existing systems, the extent of the need for changes to recently developed systems and the work that would be necessary to accomplish the changes is surprising to us and to many business users. We all question whether the techniques for defining requirements or the methods for developing systems meet the needs. A number of business users feel that one major reason for the need to change or upgrade the systems situation was the approach to system development utilized by the information services project teams in the first place.

METHODOLOGIES USED ARE OLD

The methodologies utilized at most installations of computing systems for the development of applications (other than projects for PCs) are those of the old systems development life-cycle methodology that was introduced over twenty years ago: requirements are defined, analyzed, and documented for sign-off by users; a feasibility study is conducted to evaluate the potential application and obtain approval and funding for a project; a system is designed to supposedly meet these requirements; the system is implemented; users are trained in a classroom and given an opportunity to run acceptance tests of it; and operations are converted to the use of the new system. Many application systems have been and are currently being created in this manner, according to research on corporate use of information systems, although major questions are being raised about this methodology.

Questions about Application Development Raised by Business Users

- Why is documentation usually out of date, incomplete, and difficult to use when upgrades are attempted?
- Why are requirements so often misunderstood or incomplete? Why is the system not what we expected?
- How can projects or systems activities supposedly be completed for systems that cannot be placed in operation?
- Can users not become more involved in specifying requirements, aiding more in the systems design, and finalization of processes, screens, and reports to avoid problems?
- Why is it not possible to use some of the design already available for the industry or the application being considered (chart of accounts, bills of material processing, etc.)?
- Why does application software on PCs, even complex software, seem easier to obtain and put into use than in-house applications?

These questions indicate that many business users believe they should become more involved in application analysis, redesign, and development. They seek easier means to review requirements and respond to what is being developed to meet their needs. They also want to be able to review what other companies are doing and what application designs are available for their industry or niche. One of the reasons for the increasing popularity of systems integration is that vendors who offer this service are beginning to address the desire of users to review application needs and systems more closely than ever before. It is also the reason re-engineering has gained momentum; that is, users can understand processes and can contribute if allowed. Why is this so?

Users' inherent involvement is feasible because we are dealing with the familiar processes they perform on a daily basis, and many times over and over on a daily basis. What is a process? A process is a series of steps or tasks that are performed to produce something. It is the objective of a process that it produces something of value. It may be expressed as a formula: input + value added = output to a customer (internal or external). Processes have been defined as everything we do. They are, more often than not, repetitive in nature, and herein lies the opportunity for re-engineering, cost savings, and increase in value added.

Processes may be very encompassing, as the distribution process that is made up of subprocesses illustrates.

Distribution

Receiving

Quality inspection

Put-away

Rejection process

Picking

Handling

Shipping

Invoicing

Other processes may be the following with their subprocesses.

Product Design

Logic design

Component design

Material design

Tool design

Cost analysis

Prototyping
Release to market

Product Management

Engineering change notification
Development process control
Product life cycle monitoring

Financial Management

Account control
Ledger control
Accounts Receivable

- Customer file maintenance
- Setting receivable
- Applying cash
- Aging process
- Accounts payable
- Vendor file maintenance
- Payment cycle

Production Control

Work-in-process
Work centers
Shop floor
Routing maintenance

Processes have attributes that make them easily identifiable. Processes are answerable to the following questions:

- What triggered the process?
- What should be done to it?
- How do I do it?
- What do I do next?

We would never consider hiring employees without training them or at least telling them what they are supposed to do. This is the process we define for our employees and workers. Processes should

- Be assigned to someone who is responsible for their completion.
- Have a scope normally within a larger context.
- Have receipts or inputs.
- Produce products and services or outputs.
- Have procedures or work steps associated with them.

They should also add value, be measurable, and be supported by documentation, and if necessary, corrective routines when the process falters.

Therefore, business processes are easily identified by users—they own them. Business processes separate users from information services—users understand them better. So when re-engineering is heralded by top management in response to Michael Hammer, the users can feel a renewed sense of optimism; we are now playing ball on their field.

ACTIVE USER PARTICIPATION

Business users will, we believe, participate more in analyzing business processes and subsequently become more involved in developing new and corrective application systems. The advent of PCs may have advanced this. Some application systems users implement on PCs can approach the complexity of application systems developed for minis. These systems may be developed by users with various software tools or be based on software packages that were evaluated and acquired by users, modified by vendors under the management of users, tested, and installed with formal training programs in much less time and at much less cost than applications of similar size on larger computers. The methodology used to carry out projects that develop business processes for PCs is much simpler than the old systems-development life cycle. This may contribute to a new awareness of the power of the computer and an awareness of the potential to re-engineering processes.

The techniques that have been incorporated in PCs software application packages during the rapid growth and use of PCs over the past five years have made these PC-based applications easier to review, learn, and use than applications developed for larger computers. Although the idea of user-friendly software existed before the tremendous surge of PC usage, these techniques of menus, windows, help screens, and graphics have been associated with and promoted by the PC industry. Many of these techniques should be introduced in mainframe and minicomputer packages, making them increasingly easier to evaluate and understand. We have observed this phenomenon at some software vendors, but not at the larger hardware companies that provide applications software without the aids we need to review, understand, and implement them successfully.

The use of PCs has increased the popularity of simple solutions, and we must give Apple the credit here. Many business users learned to reach for distributed or isolated solutions to problems using PCs. Even if these solutions have been chiefly spreadsheets, word processors, or databases, a feeling has been engendered that there is a lot of software available that may help a user do his or her job better and that the information services function perhaps is not the mystery it has been held to be.

The number of PCs, as we all know, has grown rapidly during the past five years, and there is now systems and applications software available for almost all industries. In view of the wealth of application software packages available, it is not surprising their use is considered so often in current application processing. There are, however, very specific reasons why the use of application software packages is considered, and re-engineering of existing processes appears another logical approach to improving the enterprise's competitive position.

In the survey we conducted, we asked companies that were considering re-engineering, Why not use available technology if all this software is available at rapidly decreasing costs? We found the following. Users want to re-engineer first and then evaluate software.

Reasons for Re-Engineering before Using Available Software Packages

Reason	Frequency of Mention
Uniqueness of company needs	Medium
Difficulties in comparing needs to package specifications	High
Packages are poor in quality	Low
Not sure of vendor's future	Low
Not sure of vendor's plans for updates	Low
Vendor doesn't provide adequate service	Low

NEEDS VERSUS SPECIFICATIONS

The major reasons for evaluating and looking at existing processes before considering vendor software involve possible differences between the needs of users (which may be unique) and the specifications of packages. The methods used to compare needs and specifications is critical to identification of the problem. When application software packages are investigated and acquired for larger computers, the process or methodology generally used at most computing installations involves evaluating needs and specifying requirements, then comparing them to the software product before proceeding with other activities required by the systems life-cycle methodology to implement the application package. The steps and time involved in this process have not proven successful, and a bad taste lingers in the mouths of users.

Re-engineering seems to be a more permanent approach. A remote PC application seems to be considered a stop-gap solution. But most important, information services is concerned with losing control over data and the integrity of the critical files—and believe us, the auditors share this valid concern.

So where does this leave us? We are left with a very good alternative, which is to rethink the whole process of how we do business or re-engineer the business process. Capabilities are available to help evaluate and install application processes and to enhance the opportunities for systems to be modified or integrated more easily.

Business users report that graphic or visual review techniques and tools (identified as one important development of the Ways of Working) have been used by Computer Associates, for example, to provide users more ability to review how systems work, are modified, and are used. In addition to Computer Associates, we have Ross Systems, the former Cullinet Software, and other vendors. The use of expert systems is also being considered by several vendors to help steer users through the evaluation and modification of application packages to meet their needs.

Process reusability is being evaluated and introduced to allow application systems to be combined with each other and with internal software to meet user needs. When the growth of useful means to modify and combine application software with internal software is considered, together with the use of graphics tools to reduce the redevelopment effort of internal applications, there appears to be credence in the conjecture of Edward Yourdon that over 95 percent of application development work will be maintenance in two years. Maintenance would change from an effort associated mostly with error correction to enhancement and re-engineering of existing code—finally the time may be right for re-engineering code (but not that old COBOL stuff). Users may be able to benefit from the fact that much of their company's business development work may duplicate work that has been done and might be available. This is where the consultants could provide invaluable insight. Banks, brokerage houses, manufacturing companies, and other organizations have bought application software from each other during the past five years. Millions of manhours of effort on design have been completed in this country and abroad. Why can we not reuse design efforts? What better use of consultants than to share a database of comparative feature, functions, and proven solutions? We will see that consultants have a valuable role in the re-engineering process, but that role is not to document current systems at a high cost and little return.

ADVANCED MANUFACTURING RESEARCH

Advanced Manufacturing Research (AMR) in Boston, Massachusetts, has—with the consulting firm of Pittiglio Rabin Todd & McGrath—set up a Supply Chain Council to develop standards and a model for the supply chain function. Supply chain is the business process of planning for manufacturing of products, sourcing materials, manufacturing a product, and distributing the completed product—in other words, of the entire manufacturing process. The

CURRENT STATE OF BUSINESS PROCESSES

supply chain model will define the basic alternatives available to its council member manufacturing companies. The model will include the following:

1. Definition of each of the twenty to thirty business processes in the supply chain and flow charts of each process.
2. Process metrics, which are common measurements to evaluate the effectiveness of alternative ways of accomplishing processes; for example, the metric to evaluate methods to complete an order may be response time, electronic data interface (EDI) as a percentage of total orders, and so forth.
3. Benchmarks, which are performance criteria.
4. Industry best practices, which are compilations of experience of manufacturing companies related to the business processes and procedures.
5. Software requirements to satisfy each benchmark and best business practice and the available vendors (e.g., Ross Systems) who develop the recommended software.

The AMR approach recognizes that there is, in fact, commonality of systems and business processes even among divergent companies, including Allied Signal, Xerox, Hoffman-LaRoche, and Johnson & Johnson. Furthermore, by capturing and defining these common business processes, AMR and the Supply Chain Council members can

1. Establish benchmarks for implementation and measurement.
2. Recommend the best ways of working with best practices scenarios.
3. Communicate processes to members, and members can communicate with distant divisions and subsidiaries.
4. Re-engineer and implement changes and enhancements.
5. Train in a constant environment.

We think AMR has validated the Ways of Working approach. They communicate this model using Ways of Working software from the COBRE Group. This selection of Ways of Working clearly indicates the advantages of the following:

1. Graphics presentation of business processes.
2. Decomposition from the top level overviews to business process detail to user processes and procedures.
3. Iterative, what-if capabilities.
4. Multiple view capability (e.g., from functional best practice, organizational, or regulatory points of view).

The Supply Chain Council members may view the model and configure its component parts to reflect how they, the members, operate in their own environments. Consultants and system integrators should try this common sense approach.

CONSULTANTS AND SYSTEM INTEGRATORS

The research study mentioned previously uncovered users who felt they had been involved in the development of redundant systems. Tools that enable existing application work to be reviewed and modified more easily could lead to much more use of development work done elsewhere and in new development efforts. One of the attractive features of the type of professional service work known as systems integration is the review of existing industry applications that users gain through the vendors who suffer this service. The growing use of systems integration and consulting is encouraged by the realization that there are applications and knowledge available in most, if not all, industries that corporations can use. Systems integration, as discussed previously, consists of integrating software packages, hardware products, and other information services together with needed modifications into an application solution for a client. Vendors who offer this service should have knowledge of many packages that could be useful in industries they serve. There is, in fact, commonality between applications of the same type that is beneficial for systems integration and for the newly emerging implementation engineering tools which are critical for success.

The market for systems integration is increasing from a revenue level below $400 million in 1980, when it was almost entirely in the federal government, to a level of over $8 million in 1990, when revenue from commercial business was significant. The capabilities of systems integration vendors that appeal to many users include a knowledge of software that is currently utilized in the user's industry: the ability to evaluate, modify, and install complex software in the user's environment; and the ability to help users walk through the use of options and potential solutions that are suited to their applications and problems. The best consultants and integrators simply must have a repository of business processes and proven solutions. We will recreate the wheel once again if we do not use this potential where it exists.

Capabilities of Systems Integration Vendors That Appeal to Prospects

- Knowledge of industry and of current problems.
- Experience in solving similar problems.
- Ability to walk through problems and possible automated solutions with users.
- Ability to provide a total solution for the user, including hardware, software, and capabilities for modification, installation, and training.

These capabilities illustrate one of the best means by which users can become more involved in process re-engineering. In addition to becoming more involved in large projects through activity with systems integration vendors, they should take the lead in defining the way they do business now. How does the process work, that is, our Ways of Working. It never made sense to have an outside consultant or integrator, at $1,200 to $2,500 a day, document the business process that you—the user—know best. Users complain that the consultants are just picking their brains and writing down their ideas. We agree with the user—but the user is to blame. Who hired the consultant to do this job? Consultants have their valuable role in process re-engineering; that role is not to do the user's job of explaining his or her business process.

WHAT ABOUT RE-ENGINEERING?

The application development required to support user and corporate objectives is generating more need for support of complex systems. For instance, the increasing need for network capabilities to support contact with customers, suppliers, and remote offices, as well as internal systems for manufacturing or other purposes, is having an impact on software support services provided by internal information services. The cry for user-friendliness and graphic user interfaces is loud. The data resource requirements of corporate plans are having a similar impact. In addition, the development capabilities and operating systems software required to support corporate plans must be managed and supported. Information services will become increasingly involved with supporting the corporate network, user interfaces, and data resources, and less involved with application development. This means users will take up the slack and must, therefore, have the tools and methods to accomplish the task.

So we see a dynamic change in the role of information services and a void in the design and definition of process requirements. The void will be filled by users because they are playing on their own field and have a means to communicate intelligently with technical information services personnel for the first time.

CONCLUSION

The current business process environment is characterized by trends that will have an impact on both information services and users in the future. For instance, users will increase their roles in development at a time when the total amount of development in terms of new application systems generated per year will probably increase. User activity will be at a high level and increase as business users continue to review (if not intensify) their analysis of application requirements and re-engineer business processes. They will analyze how existing systems accomplish work to modify and better adapt systems to meet changing business requirements. This is possible because users will have access to simplified, graphic methods of reviewing applications and designing changes to them. Users will now be able to communicate, using our Ways of Working, with the technical information services staff. Consultants will assume their rightful role as advisers, innovators, and thinkers, rather than documentalists of what is.

The information services role will change as users begin to pick up the slack of requirements definition and systems design. The information services role will increasingly become technical in evaluating better means to process data using advanced data management capabilities and new network and user-interface facilities. They will also concentrate more effort on productivity tools, re-engineering software, and technical excellence for its user base.

Both users and information services will rethink reusable design that is available today and will launch a new era in multimedia capabilities and a shift to the graphic presentation of our Ways of Working. The AMR Supply Chain Council, with its manufacturing models, has given new credence and validity to the concept of business process definitions recommended herein. Furthermore, the validity of a knowledgeable user community assures acceptance of this common sense.

5

The Status of
the User—Technically

Business process evaluation and review should not be a manual process. Wall charts are not the way to go. Practitioners should be mildly PC-literate, and do you know what? They are today. This is the status of the users—technically. They are called *technocrats*.

It is a fact that software tools have had some limited impact on activities of business users for almost twenty years starting with the use of packages on timesharing. The most popular software packages utilized by business users on timesharing in the 1970s were the financial modeling packages, which were predecessors of the spreadsheets now so popular on personal computers.

Application packages were also used on timesharing. They presented many users with the first alternative to the development of applications for in-house systems. The use of these application packages helped to spread the concept of user-controlled automation and led to the use of packages by users on mainframes, and even more so, on minicomputers. At first, the applications on timesharing were primarily batch applications that ran after users supplied input data on terminals (remote batch). The best examples, even today, are the payroll applications from vendors, such as Paychex in Rochester, New York.

In the 1970s, many timesharing applications developed on-line capabilities that enhanced their attractiveness to users. These features were duplicated on the minicomputers introduced in that period and helped to sell many minicomputers in user areas. The rising interest and use of application packages during that period also helped to make packages of interest to information services groups and top management. The progression of use of software packages and the ultimate impact on management was evident in the explosive growth of Digital Equipment Corporation, Data General, and Hewlett-Packard in the 1970s. What was really happening was the beginning of on-line processing and the demise of batch processing.

The progressive impact of vendor software and the new on-line processing was quite sequential and was a forerunner of the introduction of users to technical aspects of electronic data processing and the computer. This historical sequence occurred during the 1970s and into the 1980s. Software and on-line processing influenced the increased awareness of technology as the computer became more accessible. Still, it is arguable that users, and particularly management, were not knowledgeable in computers and data processing. Many feared computers. More were in awe. Management abdicated its role in the realm of information services. The mystique was promoted by IBM, and intimidation was common. This was to change.

THE NEW USER

Application development tools, such as report generators, modeling packages, and word processing software, were introduced on minicomputers in the 1970s and spurred interest in what could be done with computing by end-users. However, the full impact of technology on users was not felt until PCs and a cornucopia of PC software appeared in the 1980s. Surprisingly, we found business users busy at work with an assortment of vendor software packages and tools; no modern office is without its personal computers—and not terminals attached to big mainframes.

Today, the impact of technology begins in high school, if not grammar school. At the latest, it begins on the job when new hires or trainees begin to use word processing packages, spreadsheets, or database packages on PCs. The mystique began to vanish in 1990. Users have learned to program in many cases. These experiences make it easier to consider acquiring software tools to solve business processing problems or to set up small systems to keep track of customer contacts or process data for local purposes. Budget, sales, and customer data have been keyed into spreadsheet packages, such as Lotus 1-2-3 and EXCEL, and into PC databases, such as dBase III and IV, Dataease, and Paradox, to meet local planning needs or prepare special reports that can have corporate-wide impact. A department may use these powerful tools to prepare comparisons of customer revenues versus costs or reports of special opportunities identified by analysis of customer characteristics.

The ability to spend time locally manipulating data with powerful software tools, such as spreadsheets, leads to impressive results for a growing majority of business users who are seizing the opportunity. There are now many situations in which the results by business trainees are impressive, and now the growth is spreading to graphics and desktop publishing packages. These software tools can produce reports and multicolor charts in a relatively short time. In addition to the brave new world of accomplishments on PCs that is driven by the increasing capability of software tools, availability of PCs, and the shrinking costs of hardware and software, there are tools which users are acquiring that open up new vistas. These are the multimedia-based tools, such as the implementation tools that allow users to communicate effectively with the information services group and stake their claim to a role in the re-engineering strategy of the enterprise.

Business users can become major users of software packages and tools. Not only do they acquire many packages for personal computers and work stations, but they can be more and more involved in the acquisition of solutions for all sizes of computers. Users report that they assist in: the acquisition of application packages—such as accounting or manufacturing packages—to run on PCs, minicomputers, and mainframes; tools, such as word processors, desktop publishing packages, spreadsheets, and database packages, to run on PCs; software to help them use terminals on minicomputers or mainframes in their day-to-day work; and tools to develop applications. These are now within the technical realm of the end-user and are no more the sole purview of the technical information services staff. Corporate management is often surprised at the high level of software utilized by business users in their companies. The wide range of packages that a sample of business users in larger companies report they use is impressive:

Types of Software	Frequency of Mention by Companies
Word processing	Very high
Spreadsheets	Very high
Decision support systems	Medium
Graphics and multimedia	Low
Databases including query and report languages	High
Network including LANs	Very High
Project management software	Low
Fourth-generation languages	Low
Business applications (PC-based)	High
Computer-based training	Low
Expert systems	Low
CASE tools	Low
Specialized word processing	Medium
Publishing software	Medium

Information services used to be the only master of technology. Not so now. Business users justify the acquisition and utilization of software tools, not only as a means of meeting needs in their departments, but also in terms of productivity improvements they had obtained by meeting needs themselves with software tools and languages. Spreadsheets are frequently used, and remain the most frequently used software other than word processing. Business users employ spreadsheets that enable them to develop applications which would have taken the information services staff of their companies over ten times as long to handle with traditional development approaches.

Users at most progressive enterprises use software engineering techniques, with the aid of their information services staff, to generate certain types of applications over ten times as rapidly as with traditional programming languages. Numerous business users have been active in projects that used software products to design solutions to problems. Representatives of a group of companies also noted that they had saved years of project time as well as money by using vendor software applications.

This sample of experience indicates that the availability of software packages should encourage business users to become more active in application design and, in some cases, to assume actual responsibility for it. It means they are now prepared to take the lead in business process re-engineering studies. Business users' participation in application design is possible because of the introduction of new development tools and techniques and the substantial savings in time and cost, as well as potential improvement in application systems that meet business needs. As a result, many business users cannot understand why some information services–oriented projects take so long for information services to accomplish and why it is necessary to follow cumbersome procedures to solve problems. The conflict, which has raged for years, continues. It will not be an issue in business process re-engineering because users will assume a central role in the process.

The question posed now is commonplace: Are you PC-literate? The answer now, more often than not, is, Yes, I am. You will not find a graduate of an engineering school (MIT, Cal-Tech, Georgia Tech, etc.) that is not an "expert." Even older people are reading *DOS for Dummies* and no longer feel intimidated or in awe.

USERS AND BUSINESS PROCESS RE-ENGINEERING

The initial participation of users in application re-engineering is a result of the many learning experiences of the early use of computing. However, the enormous availability of books, learning tapes, and schools will lead to an even more sophisticated user in many companies, and the development of a *modus operandi* with the information services office that may leave users in charge of a major share, if not all, of application re-engineering processes. In most organizations, corporate-wide systems remains the responsibility of information services, but re-engineering will become more and more the responsibility of business users. This change is partially due to the availability of less costly hardware and software capabilities that can be employed more easily by users—Windows, graphic user interfaces, and the concept of distributed processing, which was explored exactly ten years ago by this author (Breslin). The current importance of that concept cannot be overemphasized in the growing need for user involvement in the re-engineering process. We call it client–server now, which is downloading the operations while centralizing (more or less) the computing power.

The availability of software tools that business users can employ or promote to shorten the time and work required to generate business process improvements and solutions has been increasing during the past decade. Windows are everywhere and users are becoming more familiar with this environment of tiling, imaging, and multiprocessing.

To reiterate, the rapidly growing interest of users in software tools and capabilities is related to the greater involvement of user business areas in the day-to-day use of information services. Large, corporate-wide applications that handled jobs such as payroll, accounting, and budget remotely at a central location have been replaced or augmented with applications that are running on smaller distributed computers or on terminals within departments, work areas, and offices. Computer Associates, for example, markets a network management system which epitomizes improvement of the user with the direction of information services. The system uses sophisticated software that allows the network administrator to control the network with extremely tight security. Users can be designated for systems, and security is controlled, so that payroll may be distributed remotely without fear. Data entry is the obvious extension for this process. Accounting departments, order entry units, manufacturing processes, human resource departments, and other operations have all become increasingly in charge of the local use of computing. The client–server concept has arrived. Here, a mainframe server handles the number crunching and storage of data, but the processing is local (client).

Spreadsheet packages on PCs can provide the means to solve both simple and complex problems. Budgets, financial plans, portfolio management, manufacturing planning, and other applications are being developed by users with spreadsheets and the macrostatements, templates, and various facilities now available with these software packages. A sample of these solutions revealed that many applications developed rapidly with spreadsheets took project teams much more time to accomplish in the past. This has encouraged a new class of software entrepreneurs within the corporate structure.

Alone or with the aid of information services, users are increasingly utilizing database query, reporting, and fourth-generation language software (as well as spreadsheets) to develop and run systems handling or utilizing a significant amount of data to solve many business needs. They are getting as sophisticated as the software itself, and are working on hardware that is at an almost giveaway price today. The new database capabilities on PCs, such as dBase III and IV, Paradox, and Dataease, have also been employed by users to develop applications that once would have been developed by an information services project team for a large computer.

ITERATIVE PROCESS

The increasing use of software tools and productivity packages has had an enormous effect on the approaches to development of solutions and project management that have been employed. When users employ spreadsheets, database packages, and other software on their computers, particularly on their PCs, to develop a problem solution, they have tended to follow an iterative approach to generating the solution that is similar to prototypes. A trial solution to meet business needs is developed and tested with data and then the trial solution is modified until the tests are satisfied. This iterative process is key to the successful implementation of a re-engineering project.

This process is very comfortable for users to follow. The description of requirements can be rethought during testing. If the user wants to change them or experiment with them during development, it can be done. It is difficult, after experiencing this process with PC packages, for users to appreciate why complex, formal development methodologies are required for business problems handled by the information services group. This may not be justifiable, but it is most definitely a reality to be faced by information services today.

In effect, two very real results of using software tools and applications may be to make business users more interested (1) in participating in the development of application re-engineering, and (2) in less elaborate approaches for undertaking these studies. Business users need approaches that will make it more possible for them to participate in specifying and designing a business process. This interest is being addressed, on a very limited scale, in a few organizations with the use of prototypes that allow users to simulate their application needs with a model solution. Techniques such as walking through functional or business models of a system are being used, but are generally expensive and time consuming. For this reason, CASE tools, designed for modeling, have not been overwhelmingly accepted. Some enterprises—and only the largest—are experimenting with JAD in an attempt to get more users involved. The problem here, as we discussed earlier, is that most often, the tools used in CASE and the methodology generate data-flow diagrams, and we know that users do not understand them. In almost all cases reviewed, this approach backfires and then dies. No one wants to review data-flow diagrams they do not understand.

One means of making the re-engineering projects reasonable endeavors for large companies is to incorporate multimedia capabilities into the systems life cycle. With multimedia applications like Ways of Working, users can document requirements and participate in the analysis and design of new processes. The use of multimedia methods on PCs has opened up enormous potential for involving users in the design process. Multimedia must, of course, be user-oriented and less costly than developing complete models and prototypes—or the user will not accept it as a means to a solution.

In addition to the use of new software technologies and techniques, we see a shift to a more iterative application development process. This shift is being caused by the accumulated changes in software technology during this decade, the growing knowledge of users about the use of computing, and the increasing role that business users should take in the development of computing applications. It is a shift away from methods based on "freeze frame" tasks toward the more iterative development approach discussed in this chapter. Users should review or actually describe their requirements and design business systems to achieve them by themselves in a stand-alone activity. The ability to work on application needs separately and to use tools to guide activities give business users a feeling of independence in planning and building applications.

Some of the improvement and changes in application development which would accrue with the shift toward iterative processing and multimedia technology are obvious and achievable. We use multimedia and the interative process whenever we define a business process. For example, we have described the process for getting ISO 9000 certification. (Editor's note: ISO 9000 is the process of implementing quality-oriented procedures, adhering to them, and seeking certification from a qualified auditing organization. ISO 9000 is the international standards for quality in manufacturing, distribution, and services.) With an overview, we define the five major processes required for certification as follows, each with its own deliverable or end product:

Process	Deliverable
Initial planning	Policy statement, organization
Audit and document	Quality manual
Internal assessment	Audit report
Final assessment and registration	Certificate of registration
Continued improvement	Improvement program and plan

Figure 5.1 depicts how it looks to end-users who are quality engineers and the steering committee assigned to implement ISO 9000.

Each of the processes, using multimedia, decomposes to a lower level with a more detailed description of the process. The initial planning phase, for example, exploded (or decomposed) to a process description shown in Figure 5.2. Notice that the procedures and work statements required to complete initial planning are now displayed. They are, for example, the need to define a policy, review the ISO 9000 standards, perform a preliminary survey through setting documentation control standards, and preparing a detail plan. Users can understand this step-by-step process definition. They see where they fit (or do not fit) in the process. They see the logic of the sequence and the flow of events. They see clearly where decisions are required. They see two milestones, Evaluate the Results and Review Deliverables with Management. They see the next logical process to certification is the Internal Audit and Documentation.

Furthermore, users can ask for clarification of any procedure or work statement in the process. Use of multimedia, again, allows us to decompose to more detail by procedure. For example, users may, iteratively, seek more in-

FIGURE 5.1
A Process: Overview

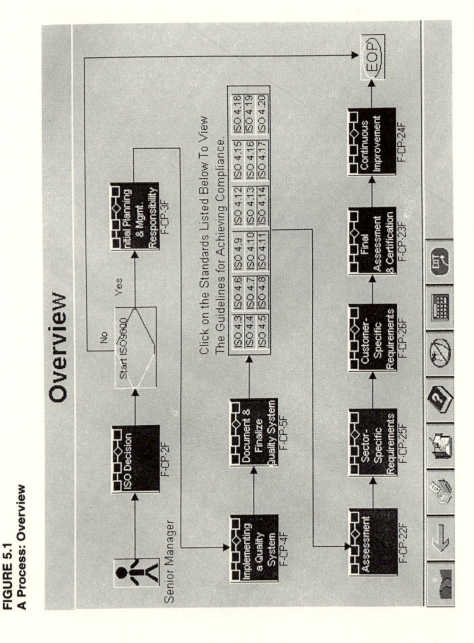

FIGURE 5.2
A Process: Initial Planning

Initial Planning & Management Responsibility

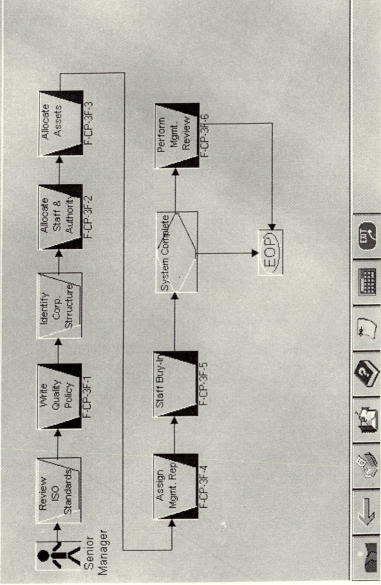

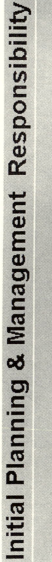

55

formation on how we define policy and implementation organization. Note that each icon is distinct. Processes look like small flow charts where procedures are colored rectangles. Each user can denote the type and nature of these icons. This is simply one example. By decomposing on that icon, we can define the procedural steps necessary to accomplish this. Figure 5.3 shows such a result as we explode down to the procedure level with both graphics and text (View Text) to define what must be done.

Users can relate to this type of requirements statement and definition of a process. The preceding indicates that now older methodologies are being altered or circumvented to provide more opportunities for users to apply their own knowledge or developments in their industries or to take advantage of new tools.

Methodologies are also being stretched and altered by information services groups and vendors to accommodate these new tools, called *implementation engineering tools*. This accommodates greater participation of users, as in the ISO 9000 example. An article in a recent technical publication suggested that the user time on several project life cycle phases be increased to provide users the opportunity to have more of an impact on the development of business systems. However, these and other changes in methodology do not encourage the full range of capabilities that are available today to be effectively used or guarantee that the business knowledge of users will be fully utilized when necessary.

ANOTHER CONCERN IS DOCUMENTATION

Along with the use of these new methodologies, a new concern arises. Users want to reduce the volumes of documentation required by system methodologies (even new methodologies that facilitate the use of structured development methods and new software engineering tools), so they can concentrate their energies on solving their business problems. This will allow them to take more advantage of their business experience in describing requirements or evaluating existing applications.

With the logic that users understand their jobs and their environments, it is a wonder that users, including managers and supervisors, are not the spearheaders of business process improvement studies. There are a series of very pointed questions that need to be answered before a re-engineering study begins. The sophisticated users are now asking them the following questions:

- How can business needs be described and reviewed more easily?
- How can the internal and external experience and knowledge in this industry be called on to answer your needs?
- How can you find out if solutions to problems are available or can be obtained through minor modification of existing applications systems?

FIGURE 5.3
A Process: The Procedure

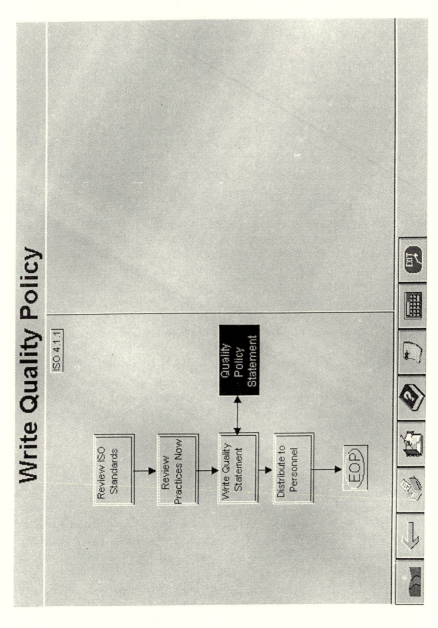

- Why can't you use more of the available technology for helping users describe their needs, review existing applications, or design solutions to business problems?
- Why can't solutions be generated more easily for all or most types of business problems?
- Why isn't it possible to utilize descriptions of requirements to help design and control the development of business applications and to help train users?
- Why isn't the design document the very essence of user documentation and training in new systems or subsystems?

These user questions can be answered with the type of approach described as the Ways of Working concept. A new approach to the systems life-cycle methodology allows a user to describe his or her situation and problems by reviewing a pictorial model of generic business activities similar to his or her own. This is better, we believe, than attempting to develop a set of written requirements resulting in a document that is too voluminous to accurately review or keep up to date. This type of approach can also facilitate development, testing, and training by making use of the graphic or pictorial model of business activities and requirements. This visual documentation has been created by superimposing information and icons on diagrams that describe the data flow or activity in existing or proposed applications, so they can be reviewed and modified easily by users. The diagrams and the changes made to them by users can also be easily reviewed by an information services organization or vendor. It requires the use of implementation re-engineering tools now available, but not well advertised.

Exploring, analyzing, and documenting requirements in lengthy narratives that attempt to define a business system was necessary when there were a limited number of applications. Now that a large number of applications have been developed, it can be an unwarranted expenditure, of time and effort, to develop a written description of functional requirements for business applications other than for the small percentage of unique ones. It is unproductive and increases the risk of obtaining incomplete or misunderstood requirements. It is also possible no one will read them, and few will understand them. One of the obvious problems that users encounter in developing requirements with older written methodologies is that they must be stated in a logical consistent manner that does not seem to relate to day-to-day business activity even when an effort is made to describe requirements in functional or business words. When this activity is carried out, system analysts or planners have to help the business user record the requirements and make sure they are precise enough to present to a technical team that will design, develop, and help the user install the business application. They are, therefore, too hard to develop.

This process often leads to a lengthy document which users find difficult to review, since they are occupied with business problems and not able to sustain their attention in reviewing a written document. According to our research, business users and management report they are much less likely to spend the time to review written documents of requirements than they were ten years ago, in view of pressures on productivity. Experience with PC software has also made them question the need for extensive documentation. Users report that there must be up-to-date documentation of applications, but it does not have to be in a written form using formats and wording that is hard to follow and often out of date. Consequently, business users have been very receptive to documentation in a visual or graphic form that can be reviewed on a display for research and planning purposes. The change to visual documentation that has been brought about by the introduction of user-oriented application development has resulted in more up-to-date documentation, since corrections or systems changes, improvement in descriptive material, and changes in business terms will be made in the course of use.

WHO KNOWS THE SYSTEM?

At the present time, many business users have to rely on information services personnel, perhaps their department systems representatives, to obtain information on existing systems from documentation and to help them prepare and make the necessary review of documentation for new applications. This situation does not ensure the knowledge of the user will be fully brought to bear on problems. In addition, it is not easy and it is sometimes impossible for users to utilize a written document to describe changes in business they want, explore the impact of changes on existing systems, record needed changes in a manner that can be used to size the effort required for development, or create information that can be used by software development tools.

The best statement on written documentation comes from a vice president of a major brokerage firm in New York. He makes a good case for information services and software vendors that the user can have an impact on the usability of systems through better documentation. He says we are experiencing the documentation barrier, the unwieldy size and structure of the printed documentation essential to using software. (We have reproduced his thoughts and words verbatim from a magazine article. This vice president, no longer with the brokerage firm, was not available for an interview.) He said that the sheer mass of today's product documentation is intimidating. Borland has established a new benchmark for bulk by equipping its massive C++ compiler package with a carrying handle. If volume were the only issue, you could probably overcome it through weight training and reinforced shelving. Unfortunately, the main problem is the diminishing utility of printed reference material. The scope and complexity of modern PC software have simply overwhelmed the capacity of conventional documentation methods.

Is on-line documentation the answer? What about the help structures that are standard in Windows applications? Regrettably, current on-line documentation is typically incomplete, awkward, and technologically primitive. If there is anything worse than using the clunky manuals supplied with current PC software, it is not having any documentation at all. Surprisingly, this is the case for a significant number of workplace PC users. Theft, loss, and general confusion significantly shrink the print documentation base. In most large companies, 20 to 40 percent of employees lack manufacturer-supplied manuals. An additional 5 to 10 percent have manuals that do not correspond to the current release of their software.

What do you do when half of your PC users do not have even basic product documentation? First, do not live with the situation and congratulate yourself on being frugal. Missing manuals means that complex software is underutilized. Users without documentation stick to narrow patterns of product use for fear of getting into a fix that would require a manual.

The best way to get new manuals is to upgrade your products. Publishers upgrade major PC packages about once a year. A fresh set of manuals usually comes with a new release, and this method of rebuilding supplies is relatively cheap. When upgrades are unavailable or too costly, third-party substitutes are the answer. Enterprising book publishers have produced excellent reference works for most major software packages.

Let us assume that you have an adequate supply of manuals for your PC software. The average PC user is unwilling to take more than a few minutes to traverse tables of contents, indexes, and the introductory sections in the reference manuals. The usefulness of printed documentation deteriorates sharply once manual size exceeds one-hundred pages, and multivolume documentation is almost worthless. The difficulty of searching increases exponentially with manual size because of the proliferation of subject cross references in the text. Add the intimidating effect of five-pound sets of reference manuals, and you have an effective barrier to exploring and mastering complex software.

Even if software producers could perfectly cross index and organize their reference manuals for optimal access, printed documentation cannot adapt to usage. Beyond judicious placement of bookmarks and developing an excellent memory for page numbers, not much can be done to adapt a printed manual to patterns of use—no matter how well written it is. The future of documentation technology lies in software. Unfortunately, existing on-line help systems are a far cry from what is needed to break the documentation barrier.

Ironically, Windows help data is text only. This makes it impossible to represent schematically product features or help system structure. Without a spatial model of the help system, it is hard to build a cognitive map of where to find things. The system is not adaptable or easily extensible. It does not learn. Perhaps the best that can be said for Windows-type on-line help is that it stimulates thinking about how to improve electronic documentation.

The following criteria, all within reach, would go a long way toward breaking the documentation barrier:

1. *Comprehensiveness.* Most current on-line help facilities are documentation supplements. They lack much of the material available in the printed manuals. Understandably, software publishers are reluctant to eliminate one of the last obstacles to piracy: the difficulty of making paper copies of voluminous printed product documentation. However, the competitive advantage and cost saving of paperless documentation will be powerful motivators.

2. *Graphical orientation.* A GUI is an ideal host for a graphically oriented documentation system. Users should be able to click on objects in a schematic hierarchy to select subjects. Obviously, the database should have at least the same quality and quantity of illustrative graphics that a printed manual has. But a user should be able to animate the illustrations by selecting a component to retrieve related information.

3. *Integrated tutorial mode.* On-line tutorials today are distinct from on-line help systems, but there are good reasons to combine the facilities. The assumption that on-line help is activated only by users who have completed a tutorial or other systematic instruction is nonsensical. It is appealing to offer a user the option of tutorial support in the context of an on-line help search.

4. *Active capability.* Once the user has located reference information, the system should help to act on that information. For example, the system should be able to execute commands corresponding to a feature it describes. The user should have a "do it" option in the work context from which to launch the documentation. A further refinement would be the capability to create stored procedures or macros based on features uncovered during a documentation search.

5. *Customizability.* Why should the help system present the same face to every user? Certainly an advanced system should have a common default mode, but it should also accommodate user preferences for search methods and display formats. Because the scope of the on-line documentation will be exhaustive, users must be able to select level of detail. They should also have the option to suppress irrelevant components.

6. *Extensibility.* It is natural for a user to annotate the documentation. This capability is strangely absent from current on-line help. Ideally, the user should be able to insert text and graphic material anywhere, with annotations distinguished from vendor material.

What can you do to hasten the demise of the documentation barrier? You can make it a priority with software vendors. Tell them that the productivity of their products is a function of how well users can learn them. Vendors must understand that pumping up the features of a product without a corresponding investment in documentation support is a dead-end strategy. Once they know you consider advanced on-line documentation a key product feature, you can be sure that help will come your way.

SAP has seen the light. The COBRE Group is developing systems for Ross Systems and Computer Associates, to mention only two. Furthermore, we believe the alternate method to long narratives is utilizing visual or graphic documentation that has been introduced to address these problems. It allows business users to look at a visual representation of the business functions they would like to improve with automation (e.g., order entry, accounts payable, and standard cost). The visual representation should include not only automated systems, but manual procedures as well. The users can see where steps should be performed differently and make changes on the display screen to make the drawings conform to their present or planned operations, as well as change the names that were being used to describe the operation. The result is a template—for users and information services alike.

Changes in the visual documentation can be recorded and reviewed by information services personnel. These personnel or vendors should perform the review after the user planning activities in order to minimize the effect on business planning. Software tools, including expert systems, can provide guidance during the user planning session by providing messages in relation to the changes users want to make in the visual representation of business systems. The changed visual documentation can be used for development, project management, testing, training, and installation purposes.

The Ways of Working approach can be used to provide the user with the means of planning and designing changed business systems or new business activities by using pictures of manual and automated systems. This development approach is based on using visual descriptions of business environments and existing or desired applications. These descriptions could be based on vendor application packages or research by information services vendors.

The drawings are created by using analysis and design tools and graphics packages used for documentation purposes. This technique has been successfully used by a group of vendors and users to develop requirements more rapidly, with fewer misunderstood or missing items, and with far more user satisfaction about the process. The uses of this technique include designing and developing modifications to existing, large applications, as well as the development of totally new systems. Graphic or visual documentation has been prepared for existing internal application systems to provide the means for users to plan modifications. For new applications, users have employed the method to describe requirements and indicated what the new system should do (a business design).

This method has been carried out by users to modify complex accounting, distribution, and manufacturing systems with little or no aid by systems personnel after visual documentation of the complex system had been prepared and users had received minimal instruction. Users have demonstrated the ability to review and make changes to this type of graphic documentation after a few hours of demonstrations. Users who participated in a demonstration of this approach by the COBRE Group, compared it to the typical method of reviewing complex systems and found it rewarding. It can save a considerable amount of the time users would need to review written documentation and specify modifications. It can also save time in estimating projects' costs and time, implementing modifications, training personnel, and testing.

Before it was possible to work with a visual description of a system, some system developers and users argued it was too difficult and time consuming to compare the requirements of their companies to the voluminous set of specifications of a software package. The time required to develop a written set of specifications in accordance with existing methodologies and compare this document in a systematic manner with the requirements was so great that it was often faster and more economical to completely develop the application in-house. Now that visual descriptions of applications are available, it has been found to be much easier, particularly for users to review specifications or define existing business processes, as well as proposed ones. In fact, users have found it easy to make changes to the graphic or visual description to describe or specify the modifications they need in software packages. Even when business users find they need to make extensive changes to the visual description of an application software package, the description might still be unsuccessfully used as a template for describing what is needed. As the number of application requirements increases, the possibility of using a visual description of an application as a template for describing requirements will steadily increase. The benefits of using visual descriptions of applications and business functions start with the fact that business users can describe and review their application needs by themselves. Requirements will be more complete and accurate, since users have full responsibility. The development process will be expedited by supplying automated information about requirements to development tools and providing the means for more easily managing development and handling testing and training. The use of iterative thinking is enhanced. The use of multimedia is the outcome.

This entire process constitutes the application development approach that is referred to as *Ways of Working* in this book. A group of vendors and consultants are now making use of it in application development work, and it is being utilized with advanced development strategies and tools, since it provides a bridge from these capabilities to the business planning activities of business users and management.

The need for this new approach to systems and business processes seems obvious. Success in application development has not been rampant. Less than 20 percent of all re-engineering studies have been successful. Attempted solutions to the development problem and system integration have been numerous. However, as has been discussed, the information services mystique is on the wane. A new approach is needed to introduce users into business process improvement. This can most certainly be done. We have seen it from SAP, with its Business Engineering Workbench, and from Ross Systems, with its Strategic Application Modeler (SAM). We participated in its development.

6

Change and Implementation Tools

Implementation tools are not new—just improved and sophisticated, allow-ing them to be used for a great deal more than implementation. They are modelers for users that can be understood by information technologists and used by management to control and monitor change. This is because these tools define a simple thing, the way we work, as templates. One president of a large software firm told me it was just common sense. He was right.

We interviewed a consultant who was once responsible for implementing IBM's MAPICS manufacturing and financial software system. The consult-ant, a manager with a large Big-Six accounting firm, found himself with six MAPICS implementation projects going on, at one stage or the other, simul-taneously. Implementation projects normally follow a four-phase pattern as follows:

1. Write an implementation plan.
2. Write user procedures.
3. Train the end-users.
4. Convert files and go live (either beta test or full-blown).

Our consultant realized these tasks were similar at each of the six client sites. In fact, he had six plans, six sets of user procedures, six training courses, and six conversion plans. The ignominy really hit home when he realized that he had six detail procedures (work statements) on how to enter the results from cycle-counting inventory into MAPICS. The fact is there is only one way to enter the counting results into MAPICS. Worse yet, the procedures were all manual or in word processing format. There was little consistency, and the quality of the procedures varied by the quality and interest of the author. This implementation nightmare, and many others like it, became the genesis of implementation tools.

To this day, many consulting firms practice the rite of *tabula rasa*, the clean sheet of paper. They will rewrite that same cycle-counting procedure for each implementation project. The reader should make sure this practice is ended. If your consultant supports its proposal with a list of clients for whom he has assisted in implementation, it is reasonable to expect that generic procedures are documented and in his possession. Jeff Culverhouse of Systems Conversion Ltd. in Cartersville, Georgia, is a major value added reseller (VAR) and consultant for Computer Associates. He implements Computer Associate's CA-PRMS manufacturing, financial, and distribution system running on the AS400. He brings a set of templates called PowerBench to every assignment. PowerBench includes all functional processes and each procedure (work statement) generically. PowerBench is Jeff's implementation tool. In fact, Jeff will tell his clients that he will not pursue any implementation effort without the templates in PowerBench.

The implementation tools have some specific features that make them useful for change management and the other objectives mentioned previously. Some of these features, common in all, would include the following:

1. *Graphics model visability.* The tools define business processes as what to do and procedures as how to do it. These processes are in the form of templates of common practices, such as receiving, shipping, and so forth, and in fact, all of the processes defined in Chapter 4.

2. *Navigational ability.* This is the ability to view the template from any number of views or perspectives. The best tools are organized in a hierarchy cascading down to more levels of detail. Then, once in place, users may navigate to detail from function, organizational, and regulatory (audit) perspectives to name only a few.

3. *Training component.* This is the ability to train on-line based on the completeness of the business process definition. The processes, therefore, should be defined to the work statement (how to) level to be in sufficient detail to allow on-line training. This is sometimes referred to as "down to the enter key." It is important to notice that these implementation tools facilitate training as a byproduct of defining your Ways of Working—a valuable and cost effective byproduct.

4. *Repository.* Business processes and underlying work statements and procedures are maintained in the tool's repository. Having systems and processes in a central repository is a primary reason that this Ways of Working concept is so adaptable to the requirement for regulatory compliance and certifications, such as ISO 9000, FDA, and QS9000. Here again, common sense dictates that something as important as the way we work should be stored in a central data bank of systems processes; in fact, this is seldom done, which necessitates the expense of having outside consultants redefining current procedures time and time again for their particular engagement (e.g., ISO certification, disaster recovery planning, re-engineering, etc.).

5. *Change management.* The implementation tool must include the ability to change processes in the repository to reflect new processes, re-engineered processes, and recommendations for improvement (resulting from some JAD efforts). This requirement, quite naturally, requires a degree of simplicity rather than a degree from MIT.

These implementation tools can be integrated with other software tools. Powerful PCs make it possible to move critical applications off mainframe computers. Powerful, graphic interfaces such as Microsoft Corporation's Windows are common, and more applications are being built using them. Dynamic data exchange (DDE) is providing new ways to link diverse applications and data. All these new capabilities are encouraging companies to reevaluate applications and processes. In a recent survey by an independent information services firm, over 70 percent of the largest 300 companies in the country are planning or actually doing reevaluation studies. Software vendors, recognizing the trend, are expanding into applications. Computer Associates, historically a systems software developer, acquired Pansophic and ASK for their applications software for manufacturers. Oracle Corporation has aggressively entered the applications software market. Eighty percent of the money spent on applications software is for the midrange, PC, and client–server architecture.

Business process re-engineering is not new. In the 1970s, in a period of economic recession, most, if not all, consulting firms found the going difficult for their standard bread-and-butter practices. Clients in a recessionary mentality did not try to undertake long and costly projects to design, program, and implement new systems, for example. To compensate for these lost revenues and to keep the practice alive, consulting firms shifted to a new practice—profit improvement. Another name associated with profit improvement studies was, of course, cost containment. We believe these studies were the forerunners of business process re-engineering.

We also believe that business process re-engineering is a more sophisticated and disciplined approach. Quite frankly, previous consulting studies had the aura of witch hunts. We will never forget one such study that took place in the South by a then Big-Eight accounting firm. The initiator was a venture capitalist firm which thrust the management services division on the unsuspecting manufacturer. The study was swift and devastating. The absurd conclusion—eliminate staff, including the quality control staff. The result was that quality deteriorated, reputations suffered, and one year later, the quality function was reinstated.

A more sophisticated approach with re-engineering would have concluded that quality should be built into the design phase. The after-the-fact quality checkers may have been reduced, but the emphasis would be shifted to the premanufacturing processes as Demming recommended so passionately for so many years. Our management services expert might have recommended this and saved more money in rework and destruction of finished goods than he did in eliminating some jobs.

Re-engineering needs to be more sophisticated. It involves using technology to design new business processes to improve productivity, performance, and in the private sector, profits. What is new is to tie business processes with information services and technology to improve the former by maximizing use of the latter. It is said that the goal here is to have the best processes integrated across functional lines, rather than compartmentalized as we have historically known. According to Hammer, users are relying on processes rather than functions as the focus of their organizations, and the human element is critical.

Key players in re-engineering studies are the ones we have identified previously; for example, the users, management, information services, and outside consultants. The latter have a very important role in the process and may be divided into three distinct categories:

Category	Examples	Approach
1. Hardware Vendors	IBM	Hardware and communications
	DEC	
2. Designers	Price Waterhouse	Systems designers from requirements to implementation
	Andersen Consulting	
	Deloitte & Touche	
3. Strategic	McKinsey	Organization, corporate and management direction
	Boston Consulting Group	
	Coopers & Lybrand	

Each is applying its strength to the broad definition of the term business process re-engineering. The strengths would be hardware and equipment, systems design, and top-level enterprise strategy. We are sure that each is objective in its approach, but caution should be exercised in retaining vendors who may not know competitive solutions and certainly have no incentive to promote them. If affordable, it would be intriguing to have a little of each; for example, a top level strategic review by McKinsey, a systems design from Price Waterhouse, and equipment and communications protocol from Digital Equipment Company.

Each, however, brings two necessary components to the study—facilitation of change and a repository of experiences. Business process re-engineering is change; change in the way we think, the strategies we employ, and the way we do things on a day-to-day basis. Consultants are change makers. It is change that justifies their existence and rings the cash register in their home offices. They recommend change, and more often than not, are excellent in bringing change about.

Consultants should also have full repositories of experiences in business processes and what works and what does not work. Otherwise, why in their proposals and boiler-plate presentations do they list their clients and write case studies of completed engagements? The implication is clear that the consultant has extensive experience in similar industries, facing similar problems. Therefore, it is reasonable to assume that this consultant will be qualified to understand your process, redefine it, and achieve the results you are seeking.

The only potential drawback from the repository argument is a real one. Often, the consulting firm has, in fact, performed the study it describes, but the consultants assigned to your engagement did not perform it, nor are they even familiar with the cited study. In larger firms, those doing re-engineering studies are younger, less experienced juniors. This is a very common problem. The study is real, but was performed many miles away by consultants not assigned to your study. Large consulting firms, from our experience with them, do not do a credible job of cataloging studies and capturing the best approaches and results in each. No one can argue that one Big-Six firm we know implemented exactly the same system in the same industry six times in one year with no sharing or comparing of feedback, collaboration, approach, benefits, or solutions to common problems.

There are several issues that must be addressed in the process of undertaking business process re-engineering. These include who should initiate the study, how to start it, and who will participate.

INITIATOR

One interesting aspect to business process re-engineering is who will initiate it and who will take the lead in making sure it happens. From all reading materials about Michael Hammer, it is clear that he believes the lead must start at the top. The initiator is normally a visionary with a propensity for change. This author knows personally that David Kerns of Xerox was such a visionary. He returned that corporation to a quality-oriented enterprise that came back to challenge all its competitors, here and abroad. We would place Lawrence Bossidy, Chairman of Allied-Signal in Morristown, New Jersey, in the same category of visionaries.

Hammer points out that re-engineering is so all-encompassing that it requires management in line operations to pull it off. Frequently, support management realizes that the potential for improvement exists, but they are not in a position to make it happen. Information services management frequently find themselves in that position; that is, recognizing the potential, but not being able to assume the role of the initiator. He concludes that information services may recognize the need, but the CEO must launch the effort.

WHERE TO START

Business process re-engineering is about processes, and that is where it should start. Redefining the way one performs business functions is the critical element in this process. It is our Ways of Working. To us, there are really three important factors in starting a business process re-engineering study:

1. Set your strategy for the study, and do not concentrate on correcting areas you should not be doing anyway.
2. Determine what the critical processes are that most effect your business or service and concentrate there. Define these processes along the lines of Ways of Working.
3. Make the decision on criticality yourself, and *never* delegate that decision to a third-party management consultant.

We were asked to re-engineer a clothing manufacturer. It was obvious that the process was antiquated. There were piles of work-in-process (WIN) materials in various stages of completion. There was inventory everywhere lying on the floor. The president pointed out that they could finish an item in one and one-half days, but the time from customer order to shipment was ten weeks. What is wrong with this picture?

The product line was interesting, too, in that this manufacturer made items that completed the product line, but had no market and were losing money on an enormous and recurring basis. It was obvious we could improve the production flow and install production scheduling techniques to reduce the WIP. But why? This manufacturer was making items that could not possibly make a profit or even break even. We concluded that he should not re-engineer this production scheduling process, but get rid of it.

We did not take the assignment because management was not focusing on what was critical. We were fixing something that should not be done in the first place. The latest on this manufacturer is that they continue to lay off workers and, apparently, lose money. Re-engineering the wrong process is a deadly approach discussed in Chapter 11.

This real-life story points up another problem. We, as consultants, were being asked to set priorities when this was management's charge. Our observation, simply put, was that developing a better way to producing a losing product was probably not smart.

Where to start is the responsibility of management. How to start is probably the design of whomever is responsible for conducting the study. Start with that which is critical by listing these critical processes. That should be easy to do. The list will soon be the definition of how we do it today. Where are we? How do we perform this function?

Most companies report that they start with a functionally-oriented organization chart and a list of all the functions performed. Now we know and agree that processes should be "seamless," and not confused by organizational dictates and boundaries. Nevertheless, you must define how processes work now and then, simply in no better way than defining what you know. A recommended hierarchy may be as follows:

- Organization.
- Functions such as marketing, manufacturing, accounting, engineering, human resources, and so forth.
- Processes within functions, such as accounting processes, which are accounts receivable, accounts payable, and general ledger.
- Subprocesses within processes, such as accounts receivable subprocesses, which are customer files, invoicing, applying cash, and so forth.

This is the process of decomposing, which is to start with the big picture and break it down to its component parts and break these parts into finer parts, and so on. Before defining how each subprocess and process works, you should list them within a picture of the enterprise and the scope of the study. Here, of course, is where a methodology like the Ways of Working is so important; it provides structure to this decomposition and scope.

An alternative to getting started by organization is to catalog major inputs, processes, and outputs. Inputs are relatively easy to identify: customer orders, purchase requisitions, vendor invoices, and the like, normally start processes. People and software process them. Reports, payments, and products are typical outputs. Try this.

Practitioners report that the functional list (whether organizational or input or output based) should not be a wall chart either, for the wall chart is too inflexible and does not allow reiteration of possible alternative re-engineered approaches. The list should not be three-by-five cards either. These small cards do not allow you to see how the whole system or function works. Of course you will lose them. We do not know how you keep track of them anyway. But believe us, some companies have reported that they do use three-by-five cards to re-engineer business processes.

The initial review of processes should not take too long, according to the proponents of business process re-engineering. Hammer referred to this phenomenon as an analysis tar pit. We would comment that other advocates warn that the analysts should not throw out old processes too soon either, but should analyze them for both strengths and weaknesses. Old ideas are the basis for new ideas. Old ideas may stimulate that innovation which results in solutions to the problems that necessitated the study in the first place.

USE OF CONSULTANTS

Another issue in business process evaluations is one to which we have alluded; that is, the need to manage outside consultants if they are used in the study. Most re-engineers would recommend use of an outside opinion. Many spend millions of dollars. Coopers & Lybrand say they only want the big studies. A Coopers & Lybrand, Washington-based consulting partner was quoted as saying that Coopers was not looking for low-bid engagements. Another observation from Coopers was to the effect that they are strictly the high-priced spread. If so, the status of re-engineering should dictate that users of consultants should expect a big price tag and should be in the position to manage that effort. We would observe that Coopers may brag about their large fees, but all studies reviewed by any consulting firm results in this magnitude of fees.

The most successful studies, we observe, are those where the buyer of consulting services clearly defined the role of the consultant. The users then

1. defined the scope (i.e., business processes).
2. did the initial analysis and definition of current practices. (Who would know them better?)
3. assigned the consultant's role as the source of recommendation and comparative solutions.
4. held the consultants responsible for their recommendation.
5. prioritized the recommendation based upon criticality.

The status of re-engineering today is varied, but what seems common in the more successful efforts is the use of consultants properly, but not recklessly.

With respect to the use of consultants, a good rule is to make sure that each phase of the study should produce sufficient savings or earnings potential to justify the next phase. This is the way to manage a consulting assignment. When the benefits no longer outweigh the costs, end it.

Finally, with respect to the participant of re-engineering, the trend is toward more user involvement. The popular term today is empowerment. It is consistent with the goals of successful re-engineering projects; for example, that management manages, information services provides the technological solutions, users provide the input on how things work and how they can work better, and consultants provide experience and alternative solutions to contemplate. It is consistent with the approach taken in successful studies; for example, that management sets the targets from the top down, but users describe the how, who, and why from the bottom up. Ultimately, the user must be responsible for the operation of the system.

Where does information services fit into all of this? In addition to being an integral part of the study, information services will inevitably be asked to recommend the means of attaining the best-functioning new process and implementing that solution or corrective action. That has not changed. And because it has not changed, the very old and real shortcomings in information processing will still be with us. What has been short-written in the queries approaches is that we may cancel the process, but it must be replaced by something new or corrective. And unless something changes from the way we selected and implemented systems in the past, the re-engineered solution will fail just as the old system failed. What is needed is a new approach to the implementation of solutions.

WHERE DO WE GO FROM HERE?

How should we evaluate our business processes? This is the question being asked by management, educated users, and information services personnel alike. What is the meaning of the question? It has been discussed earlier that the history of data processing has been an evolutionary process since the period 1956–1960. That is also true of business processes. In the period beginning in the 1970s came a reasonable set of software packages to support our business processes.

Business processes are the procedures that literally are used to run companies. Management had gained a high level of awareness of computers, including PCs and software. This same level of understanding is needed for the business process that the software supports, for it is business processes that drive our factories, report our financial conditions, and measure our productivity.

The concept of re-engineering is impacting the information processing industry in the 1990s. It will encompass the segment of the systems software market used to develop solutions (Ways of Working). Software and software products can improve the exchange of information related to business processes among functional departments, management, and the information services group. Re-engineering can help to lay out the issues, demand the tough decisions, and uncover opportunities for productivity improvements. In order to get this level of expectation, however, re-engineering must be undertaken without undoing the organization.

Most information services experts agree that the selection of the right systems software tools, now called implementation engineering tools, is key to the evaluation of processes and the development of corrective systems. Statistics indicate that the average manufacturing system has a large number of functions and processes. A manufacturing system will consist of mission-critical elements, such as inventory control and shop floor control, that were long and expensive in design and implementation. The information services are forced by this sheer logic to evaluate existing systems and try to retain what they can.

Systems are big business. Software was a $2.9 billion industry in 1982, and is growing at a rate of 40 percent annually. It reached $50 billion in 1994. Several thousand software companies market 60,000 standard software packages and products. A major vendor of software advertises that it develops one new software application each working day. Some information services personnel will want to use these packages as corrective systems. But will they be prepared to evaluate these systems as improvements for existing systems? Where does the information services look for solutions? How do they translate the findings of your business process re-engineering study? The fact is that they cannot, unless the study is done properly and in a format that all can understand—the framework to communicate.

SOME ISSUES RELATING
TO IMPLEMENTING SOLUTIONS

It is often overlooked by the academicians recommending re-engineering that recommendations of re-engineered processes must be implemented. In a real-life situation, the order processing function of a major paper manufacturer required three weeks from order to shipment. We re-engineered the process recommending new order processing and entry systems. The issue then was simply how. We envisioned a long project.

It is a fact that large systems projects become ends in themselves, and that is sad and counterproductive. Systems are installed to solve problems or provide a competitive edge through efficiency, effectiveness, and the generation of information to help in managing companies. Frequently, however, because of inadequate management commitment, long project implementation, and a technical rather than user orientation, the project becomes the focal point, and the original goals and objectives are lost.

The result is bad. Money is wasted, morale is affected negatively, and expectations are shattered unnecessarily. These three problems—management commitment, long implementation projects, and the technical orientation—can and must be overcome if the recommendations of the business process re-engineering study are to be implemented.

Management commitment is attainable. It is a matter of establishing clear and measurable goals and objectives for the re-engineering study and publishing them at all appropriate levels. This is done at the onset of a project, not at the end. The key is measurability in clear quantitative terms that we all agree to and understand. Agreement comes through a written buy-off from management. The goals and objectives are inextricably incorporated into every phase of the re-engineering project from the findings to the corrective software evaluation and selection, through project planning and implementation, until postassessment of the system. To forget goals in any step along the way is to shift emphasis to the project itself, making it an end rather than a means. This concept is setting meaningful and measurable goals and objectives.

Similarly, long implementation projects are not a foregone reality. Re-engineered corrective actions can be implemented in a reasonable time frame. The better the application meets the requirements of the findings, the better the chance is for a successful and timely implementation. The enemy, ever present, is to overdesign an in-house effort and to recreate the wheel. On the other hand, packages, being generic, will never match each unique requirement of the new process. Therefore, a poor project can result where no fit exists. It is a fact that a large toy distributor is, at this time, spending more on modifying a packaged distribution system than they paid for the original package. And we are talking millions of dollars. So where is the fit?

Long implementation projects often result because adequate tools and techniques, which should be in place to assist the implementation team, are lacking. Specifically, implementation plans, conversion plans, and flexible user documentation should be available. The implementation methodology, which is different for packages than for in-house developed systems, also should be understood and in place. Where these necessities are in place, long lead times and exorbitant consulting fees do not result. The proper tools and methodology are required, during the business process re-engineering study, and to implement the new or corrective systems and processes.

Finally, a user orientation and involvement can be attained. This is achieved during the delegation of responsibilities. The buzz word here is "empowerment"; that is, he who would benefit most from the system should be responsible for it and be involved in its design. It is the user's system, not the consultant's nor the information services manager's. Failure to establish this transfer of responsibility to the appropriate users will normally lead to failures. Establishing this orientation and assuring proper responsibilities are important. Empowering the user is critical.

When processes are evaluated, information services must address implementation. Unlike the past, packaged software solutions are not going to be the only sane solution for long. Quite frankly, they have not always been successful. Until now, the alternative was not a good one, that is, in-house development. Do you know who hates packages? IBM does—and that being so, the 1990s may see a shift from packages to in-house development. More likely, we will see packages based on database design, retrieval capabilities, and client–server architecture. Ross Systems is there now. Some vendors provide the package and the source code. The system should be supported by SAM, the Ways of Working implementation technology.

The shift requires a new involvement of users and management. It truly elevates management responsibility in the previously considered mundane systems process. Management with IBM's support will no longer delegate decisions to technicians and software vendors on systems that are used to run factories, distribute products, and account for the financial health of companies. The objective is to quantify management goals, to implement corrective systems efficiently and cost effectively, and to measure the results against the preengineered expectations. This methodology helps to surface critical system's decisions, which are really business decisions. Then, using software tools and applications as the framework to communicate, the implementors present pivotal business issues responsive to re-engineering recommendations to management for direction before implementation. To complement this methodology, graphic tools are used to increase understanding and reduce the trauma of implementation and, subsequently, the cost, time, and risks of computerized systems, because re-engineering is change; no doubt about it.

So there is hope. Not only can we improve our experience in implementation, we can shift the focus from systems to the attainment of the objectives that were established by the re-engineering team and project. Software can become the catalyst for improving the overall performance of the company, and uniquely so. A former vice president of Cullinet Software in Westwood, Massachusetts, put it best. Software forms a "framework to communicate" in that it forces us to rethink every major function from pricing and commission structures to the planning and making of products we market. Ways of Working provides the tool to create that framework.

With such inherent power and potential impact, software must be evaluated as solutions to business processes. We must clearly understand when and under what circumstances systems should be implemented with in-house development and when packages may be appropriate. In some cases, it is clear that packages may be an alternative. However, the issue must be resolved, and the pros and cons of packages and in-house developed systems must be evaluated. It is the old make or buy decision.

It is really an interesting discussion, too, in that the issues that are paramount in the decision to make or buy are the same issues inherent in the difficulties experienced by companies when attempting to implement software packages using systems software products. In other words, it is the advantages of custom, in-house development that are lacking in software packages and ultimately cause the problems with packages. Interesting? We think so. Let us look at make or buy decisions for systems in today's environment. When the team of re-engineers recommend a new business process, what approaches are open to our beleaguered information services professionals? This was the dilemma facing our paper-goods manufacturer with the recommendation that we implement a new order entry system.

IN-HOUSE ADVANTAGES AND DISADVANTAGES

There is one major advantage to developing software solutions internally and several peripheral advantages emanate from it. The single most persuasive argument, it seems to us, is that the system can be designed specifically for the company and for the unique requirements defined in the re-engineering study. If properly done, the systems can be developed to reflect the specific set of functional specifications set forth by the team. It then becomes a perfect fit for the current environment and perfectly responsive to the team's recommendations.

There are several auxiliary and related benefits. First, there is no need to immediately customize the product, as the product (system) is, by definition, custom. Additionally, future enhancements may be easier to accomplish because the staff members are more familiar with the source code and the internal logic of the system that they, of course, designed and programmed. Second, and again by definition, there is the potential for intimate familiarity with the system, as the developers are on-site. Therefore, features and functionality may be better understood. Training, internally, should conceivably and logically be better, as the designers become the educators, demonstrators, and instructors. Proximity to those knowledgeable in the system is assured with proper techniques we will recommend in later chapters.

These advantages, which are fundamental weaknesses in counterpart for packages, must be weighed with any disadvantages of in-house development. In the past, the major disadvantages were the long lead times, high costs, and risks. Packages can be installed in a fraction of the time it takes to develop systems internally. Installation can be anywhere from immediate to one-quarter of the time of doing it in-house. With packages, people still remember why they wanted the system, they are probably still on the job, and they can see things being done. Simply put, these solutions can be quickly evaluated vis-à-vis the recommendations set forth by the re-engineering team.

Time is money. The longer the developmental timetable, the more resources that will be expended on the project. Furthermore, it will take longer to re-engineer the process. The extended length of time also contributes to the uncertainty of the cost. Again, the future is hard to predict, and the more distant, the more difficult, as a general rule. There has been a history of cost overruns in large systems projects in the past.

The long lead time, in addition to complicating the cost estimating, also increases the risk of failure. A major business process requires literally thousands of decisions, options, and features. Direction, in a major process, comes from many sources and organizations. It is not an easy matter to coordinate and control the many user requests and successfully develop a single process that pleases everyone; it simply is not an easy task. Consequently, there is a risk that the in-house system may not perform satisfactorily in the final analysis. Although clearly an extreme, it is well known that a major process manufacturer (a Fortune 500 company) spent three years and more than $8 million in developing a manufacturing system that never worked. Today, reeling from the experience, a complex manufacturing package is installed.

Finally, in-house developed systems to improve business processes may perpetuate and institutionalize bad business processes. Too often, designers merely automate current procedures, whether they are good or bad. This practice results from a lack of communication, and it is one of the real dangers in a re-engineering study. That is, the recommendations are for automating a bad process when the process should have been nixed.

PACKAGES ADVANTAGES AND DISADVANTAGES

Are packages the perfect solution to re-engineered business processes? There are many advantages to packages that account for the fact that this alternative is often selected by information services directors today. In contrast to in-house development, packages can generally be installed more quickly. This is elementary in that there is no need for many time consuming tasks such as

- Detailed systems specifications
- Detailed programming specifications
- Extensive programming efforts
- Extensive programming and system testing

In addition, in all major packages some training and documentation is provided to reduce the time needed to develop these essential materials. It does not, of course, reduce the time needed to train or to understand the documentation. In fact, user training takes on a new significance.

Packages then generally can be installed more quickly and, therefore, can be budgeted for more accurately. That is not to say that packages are always less expensive. Packages and in-house development both can be expensive. Nevertheless, the shorter installation time, coupled with other features of packages, may reduce the risk of failure. Packages can be installed with expectations that can be met sometimes.

Second, packages may be considered to be superior products, in some cases, to in-house development. This is a logical conclusion, too. The most successful packages in theory have been developed over a period of years by persons who should be knowledgeable in the application. They are then field tested in many installations. The most successful packages, therefore, should not have major problems, and they can be demonstrated in real life environments. This often reduces the risk of failure.

Industry knowledge may be of greater importance in specific (or vertical) industry applications. Here, the software developer has specialized in specific industries from apparel to aerospace to weaving. The most successful packages have incorporated leading-edge technology to give users that competitive edge over nonusers. It is a consideration of some importance in the make or buy decision.

The most compelling argument to managers always will be the importance of gaining a fast solution that will address the problems of the business and the goals set by management. As such, it seldom makes sense to reinvent the wheel, to spend the effort in developing a feature or system that exists, and drain resources from addressing the use of the system to meet and beat the competition and remain a healthy financial entity. In-house development to date has meant reinvention of the wheel. But what if this could be changed?

A second, and perhaps as compelling an argument for packages, comes from the information services community, which most nearly understands the issue of make or buy. They call it the *maintenance crisis*. The maintenance crisis is the fact that the function of maintaining software programs within large companies is undermanaged and understaffed. The maintenance of existing software programs consumes, on an average, over 50 percent of the total electronic data processing (EDP) budget in large companies and as much as 90 percent in some. Other observations we have made include the following:

- The average backlog of maintenance requests is almost two years. The size of the backlog ranged from a low of two months to a high of five years.
- The maintenance function is undermanned and responsibility is mostly diffused rather than being delegated to a single person.
- Nearly 80 percent of the respondents said their systems had to be maintained by specific individuals because no one else understood them and the internal logic of the computer programs.
- Most companies do not even have a formal methodology for determining which system should be rewritten, and very few require that existing systems be modified to reflect the most current standards and technologies.
- A vast majority considers maintenance programming to be an unprestigious position in the world of software programmers.

The conclusion here is that maintenance is expensive and neglected. In-house development is maintained by in-house developers, and it is reaching crisis proportions. According to one executive, maintenance is just considered an expense, a way of business. Information services have been conditioned to pay the price, and they do not yet understand there are alternatives that could drastically reduce that cost. One of those alternatives, which must be addressed in face of this crisis, is software packages that are maintained by the developing software firm. Others are better design, more user involvement, and data-oriented design, as we shall see later.

This leads us to the final consideration—the disadvantages of software packages. The major disadvantage is that the packages are generic, and not being designed specifically for the company, will require some changes. This is a change that may be made either to the software or to the way we do business, but nevertheless a change. This change will be made by users and data processing professionals, who do not intimately understand the software product they are changing or the implications of the change within the organization. This change will be made with generic and often inadequate documentation and plans. There are major uncertainties to changing software packages:

- Will the modification in one module have repercussions in another related module?
- Will we lose the vendor's support if we change this system?
- When is modification so extensive that the better solution would be to design and program the entire system in the first place? (Remember the toy distributor?)
- How do we implement future upgrades and enhancements offered by the vendor?

THE BOTTOM LINE

The bottom line is that packages have a place in this software world. It is not black and white, but grey. There simply is not a guideline that says packages are correct for this institution, while in-house development is best in that situation. There are times when a package is best for a specific purpose. For example, we believe that packages may often be applicable in a specific vertical industry, such as apparel, where several software companies have specialized in a vertical market and offer targeted solutions for the apparel industry.

Another area where packages seem best are in common, standard-directed applications, such as a general ledger system. Several software vendors market superb general ledger packages. Each has flexible and consolidated reporting, and flexible report-writing capabilities, not to mention budgeting capabilities. It probably makes little sense to undertake the cost, time, and risk to develop an in-house general ledger system as a result of a re-engineering study.

In-house systems may be best in the mission-critical systems such as Enterprise Resource Systems, which are innovative, addressing a unique situation, and resulting in a competitive advantage. Remember our toy distributor. The reason that this giant is spending more to modify the distribution system than it originally cost is probably because it simply does not fit the needs of the company. The proposed new business process was unique; the package was generic and all its competitors had one just like it. The database approach is best here. Vendors should develop the core functionality and let the users, through SQL and switches, modify the external appearance and use of the system—always supported by the Ways of Working.

ENTER SAP

In 1992, a company from Walldorf, Germany, named SAP, introduced a new and sophisticated manufacturing software package called R/3. In mid-1996, almost 500 U.S. companies were implementing SAP's R/3 system. The system is large with severity modules clustered in four major components, including financial, manufacturing, sales, and human resources. The new system has it all: a single, totally integrated architecture running on a client–server platform. The integration aspect requires that users must modify the way they work to conform to SAP's R/3. No more can we say we will either modify our processes or modify the software; the only alternative is to modify the way we work.

This is a major requirement. According to a consultant from Deloitte & Touche, the difficulty is apparently exacerbated by the complexity of the software and the lack of people that understand R/3. According to an article in *CFO* magazine (CFO Publishing Corporation, Boston, Massachusetts), implementation can easily cost $20 million and literally thousands of jobs are affected. As a result, the consultant must reexamine every affected business process on a multinational scale. Implementing SAP requires re-engineering of business processes, which is normally an excruciating experience at best. In the case of SAP, the $20 million can even reach $200 million for worldwide implementation efforts by large multinational companies. There are over 8,000 tables in the SAP database. These tables directly affect users in their daily use of R/3, as the tables determine the exact functionality. R/3 forces users to define and understand these tables and the effects of setting switches. This is the process of configuration.

According to Deloitte & Touche, 20 percent of the implementation effort is consumed in configuring R/3. The remaining 80 percent is invested in re-engineering the company to meet the system. It is this dilemma that caused SAP to create its own unique implementation tool called Business Engineering Workbench (BEW). It is important to realize that BEW focuses on the configuration. This, we believe, must be coupled with Ways of Working for re-engineering the workplace to fit R/3. Configuring the system is important. Defining how it will work is critical.

The consultants responsible for R/3 implementation should document the generic Ways of Working, so this knowledge will be carried over to subsequent clients. Hopefully, this is being done. Clearly the complexity of SAP's R/3 brought to light the need for implementation engineering tools such as BEW and Ways of Working. It seems clear that inflexible and poorly supported software would assume too much of the user. When some vendors succeeded with their inflexible general ledger and financial packages, the overzealous marketers extrapolated that success to all applications. But there were and are major differences in financial and other mission-critical systems.

Primarily, finance is an old art, standardized by time and public accounting firms, which must attest for the accuracy of the resulting financial statements. Mission critical requires flexibility and ease of understanding and implementation.

Accounting has become more standardized and more or less fixed in principle and design. Software, therefore, can be developed that will accurately and consistently produce a trial balance and a general ledger for a variety of different organizations. Similarly, accounts payable, accounts receivable, and in most cases, payroll can be developed to operate effectively in a variety of companies, industries, and organizations. Yet, the same cannot always be said of order entry, distribution, and manufacturing. Does a general solution fit the re-engineering recommendations designed to grab that competitive advantage?

Manufacturing is fixed to a lesser extent. Some principles have become standardized by a group of gurus named Wright, Plossl, and Orlicky; their writings and observations have resulted in standardizing and optimizing the techniques for the engineering concepts of bills of material and work-center processing. On the other hand, who has done likewise in pricing, marketing, distributing, warehousing, and ordering? No one.

To be sure that we have not overlooked another factor, let us also note that these latter systems require more user input from a diverse group of disciplines. Conversely, general ledger and the financials are really the domain of the controller and his or her staff. Therefore, the more esoteric applications, such as order entry, require even more user involvement in the final product and are subject to more alternatives and deviations; therefore, these applications require a better concept of documentation. Ross Systems has adopted such an approach and, therefore, greatly enhanced its users success rate and satisfaction.

Together with the arguments put forth in the first chapters, user responsibility for the design process is necessary, inevitable, and desirable. This leads us to an evaluation of the implementation tools as the means to enhance user participation (i.e., empowerment and responsibility) and the role of the user in the decision to pursue business process improvements.

7

Business Process Review and Improvement

We reiterate at this point that processes should be reviewed for improvement. But the study is not an end in itself. Information services will be charged with the process of implementing proposed solutions. They are faced with real-life alternatives. Inflexible packages arrived because marketers thought they could capitalize on the success of general ledgers and packaged payrolls. Disappointments may have often accompanied the recommendations of re-engineering to implement new mission-critical business processes. This is because the recommendation process (re-engineering) may be relatively new and vital, but the implementation process remains the same. The problem is the difficulty in analyzing processes and simplifying the implementation process as SAP management realized.

It is ironic, too, that many software vendors, when asked to solve a problem, will tell customers quite candidly that no package really fits perfectly. The goal is to achieve an 80 to 85 percent fit. What to do with the other 20 to 15 percent? That is to be handled with modifications. However, *some* vendors do not support products modified by the user's information services department. Other vendors *cannot* support products, even if they wanted to, because the users have not maintained good records of what they have changed. Ross Systems, however, provides the source code, client–server environments, and database design. SAP and Ross Systems provide the tools. Products have been introduced and companies have been founded to help users keep track of changes. It is expensive, but if users are determined to implement applications software packages and modify these packages, then they had better use some form of change control and management.

Complicating matters, of course, is the whole history of software development companies, such as Cullinet Software, once the largest in the world. Who would have thought this wonderful company would fall on hard times, lose money for thirteen straight quarters, and be acquired? Cullinet had almost 1,000 companies using its packaged software, including approximately 300 that had acquired its mission-critical manufacturing system. This system costs between $500,000 and $1 million and much more to modify it, train users to use it, and implement it successfully.

Yet Cullinet, the most successful and prosperous software developer in 1984, closed its doors in 1989, a mere five years later. More precisely, Cullinet was acquired by the behemoth Computer Associates of Islandia, New York. As this book is being published, Computer Associates actively supports Cullinet's applications software, including manufacturing and human resources. Other companies may not have. Computer Associates is aggressively updating the manufacturing system to a client–server environment and open-systems architecture.

The banking applications at Cullinet is a different example. Cullinet had invested literally millions of dollars in acquiring the Bob White banking software, redesigning the system, and recoding it almost in its entirety. A medium-sized marketing staff was in place and out recommending the Cullinet Banking System (CBS) to the largest banks in the world. Many banks spent untold dollars and hours evaluating CBS, a truly mission-critical system. At least three—and most likely five—banks selected CBS after intensive review.

Upon Cullinet's demise these major banks were left with nothing. Computer Associates, for perfectly sound financial reasons, elected to drop the Cullinet Banking System: Bob White, redesign, coding, marketing, and all.

Cullinet is simply not an isolated case. Martin-Marietta dropped its mission-critical manufacturing system. MSA, a software company in Atlanta, was acquired by Dun & Bradstreet (D&B) Information Systems late in 1989. AMAPS, D&B's manufacturing software, has historically experienced turmoil. There is simply no way for users to predict what will happen to software developers like Cullinet or to software applications packages such as Martin-Marietta's manufacturing system. The key to using packages is to stay with the more established vendors (e.g., Computer Associates, SSA, SAP, and Ross Systems), and to make sure that the support is technologically superior and on-line graphics documentation is a basic and in place.

We began with in-house developed systems, but the pendulum swung dramatically to packaged software in the 1980s. We wondered if the pendulum could swing right back in the 1990s because IBM wants it; we conclude that it will not. Why did IBM get out of MAPICS marketing then? It is important to review the problems of implementation of systems and software for business process improvement.

We can state it simply: The problem most often faced in developing new business processes is the difficulty in analyzing processes adequately and accurately. In other words, the team is not able to define a newly re-engineered process in such a way that anyone, typically information services, can implement it quickly and easily. This was because of a number of reasons including (1) communications, (2) changing conditions, (3) confusing techniques, (4) scarcity of talent and misuse of what is available, and (5) a definite lack of software development tools. Each of these key problems will be discussed because (and this is crucial) these problems must be addressed and resolved if we are to be able to implement the recommendations of re-engineered processes in a cost-effective manner and continue to be able to implement change and adapt rapidly to market-driven requirements for better systems and more accessible information.

COMMUNICATIONS

Narrative descriptions of complex procedures are not good forms of communications. Requirements statements are invariably long narrative dissertations prepared by systems analysts for the eyes of the user and, perhaps, ultimately for a software vendor. Yes, we can understand narratives in stories, novels, and travelogues, but we simply cannot do so readily in complex systems and business processes.

Narratives never seem to be in context, but generally ramble on according to some organizational theory of the analyst. Users are asked to read the volumes, put them into context of their real-life requirements for information, and approve them. Historically, this has not been possible; therefore, it has not been a successful approach. We have often said that a picture is worth a thousand words; analysts invariably produce the thousand words rather than the single picture. The brilliant re-engineering recommendations are translated into volumes of requirements. It simply destroys the potentials found in the study.

A second problem with communications between systems developers and business users is that they speak a different language. Analysts invariably resort to the alphabet with RAM, ROM, SQL, TSO and RPG. The same analyst speaks computers with bits and bytes and disks with sectors. Finally, the same analyst shows up with HIPO charts, data-flow diagrams, and decomposition charts. The user seldom knows these alphabets, computers, or the tools with which the analyst works. The users simply know what they need, what they do, and what their requirements are for a new system. They know the human interaction necessary to make a system successful, but they cannot communicate this in languages and techniques used by the knowledgeable systems analyst.

Third, communications are complicated by the newness of the proposed business processes and our inability to describe processes and procedures adequately. How often have we heard that the user could not visualize the proposed process or procedure? This observation was critical to the pendulum swing to a package solution, in which the user could, in fact, better visualize the basic concepts of the proposed new system. There is the screen, the form, and the report. In contrast, the in-house system is normally a figment of someone's imagination.

In summary, communications between information services analysts and business users is usually less than perfect. A major deterrent to good communications is too much narrative with little consideration of the graphics approach to requirements definition. Second, communications are difficult because information services technicians and business users speak an entirely different language with, until recently, no framework to communicate. Finally, communications are complicated by the fact that new processes, in the analyst's mind, are just difficult to visualize. Our favorite analyst, a brilliant Ph.D., tries to communicate his design criteria with menus and screens. The menus are too general, and screens are not only out of context, but useful only to the good doctor; but he is not alone in the inability to communicate complex procedures and business processes.

CHANGING CONDITIONS OF THE STATIC DOCUMENT

The difficulty in designing systems is the difficulty of analyzing systems properly. Communications is a problem. A second problem in this regard is the changing scope and conditions of the business process design. Unfortunately, business needs are not static; therefore, a statement of user requirements cannot be static either. Systems analysts and fixed-priced consultants hate this fact of life. They would prefer to define a period of time after which requirements cannot be changed. This, of course, fits in nicely with the old systems life cycle. Information systems analysts loved to say that we have completed the requirements phase, and now we are in the design phase, never to return to requirements.

There are major problems with this approach. In the first place, businesses and information needs do change. In this dynamic market with competition here and abroad, it is ridiculous to think that we can put a hold on the users' need to redefine their requirements. In the second place, new concepts and new ideas mean that the system design and the best means to handle a user request will also change. So requirements and potential solutions based on re-engineering change, and therefore requirements cannot remain static.

But everyone, including the experienced re-engineer, knows this. The problem is not that they do not know changes will occur; the problem is that it is too costly and too difficult to make changes. We are right back to the narrative statement of requirements. Even with word processing, it is a pain in the neck, a costly procedure, and a time consuming task to change long-winded narrative specifications and user requirements.

In the long run, freezing the requirements, as it was once called, in essence ends dialogue and prevents meaningful discussions of what is really needed in a system. The result is often a poor design, an angry user, and potential for gigantic failure. The symptom underlies the real problem in analyzing systems requirements and designing a good system as the re-engineered solution. As with the failure to communicate, this symptom necessitates a new approach to re-engineering. It means there must be a way to easily and cost-effectively maintain user requirements and re-engineered solutions.

The old theory was to freeze design while trying to create a system sufficiently flexible to allow changes in the future. This is costly. The enormous backlog of changes resulted, in some part, from this philosophy. All software vendors concur in at least one point: It is less expensive and less disruptive to identify and make modifications in the design phase than after a system is operational. This, we will soon see, is the underlying justification for the Ways of Working approach; that is, changes are better made with graphics tools than by modification of computer code.

We think, furthermore, the problem with changes reflects the fallacy of the old systems life cycle. This will be discussed later. Now to continue on the problems of business process improvements and implementing solutions, we turn to the issue of conflicting techniques.

CONFUSING TECHNIQUES

Almost without a doubt, it is correct that a single methodology is needed to analyze systems for future design and implementation of improved processes. The problem facing the re-engineer is which methodology. There has been an ongoing argument among the leading engineers of system design as to the best methodologies. The systems engineers promote data-structured techniques over process-oriented techniques. Data-structure proponents—and the terms will be defined shortly—believe that this type of approach technique is more exacting and requires more rigor than the process-oriented approach.

A methodology is an all encompassing means used to define a process. It consists of all facets of the old systems life cycle, not just symbols and rules of syntax, such as this symbol cannot logically be connected to that symbol without some intervening process (or symbol). Many people confuse the technique with methodology, and in fact, there have been historical arguments about which methodology is the most effective. But clearly, a methodology is more than a symbol; it is an approach—an all encompassing one at that.

Several very prominent software engineers are the leading developers of techniques for systems analysis. We will later discuss the differences in their approaches. One has developed a strategy called data-structured systems development (DSSD), which is an effective means to define systems in a data-oriented approach. To paraphrase a noted proponent: The purpose of logical modeling is to take vague ideas about requirements and convert them into precise definitions efficiently with graphics that allow you to lay out the basic concepts of the system. So these techniques for systems analysis are graphics oriented, but are not prototypes of the system itself.

To some, logical modeling consists of data-flow diagrams and entity-relation models, and it is an effective way for system analysts to analyze and document a system previously only resident in their minds. According to some system engineers, the process is logically broken into phases:

- *Phase 1.* Develop a systemwide data-flow diagram (DFD) describing the underlying nature of a system.
- *Phase 2.* List the data elements to be stored in each file (data store) as defined in the DFD.
- *Phase 3.* Determine what entity-relationship exists in the structure of the data to be stored in the system.
- *Phase 4.* Describe the model (normalization).
- *Phase 5.* Rethink the DFD to reflect a complete view of the system and its data as a result of entity-relationship analysis and normalization.

This approach seems well suited for the system analysts and most certainly puts discipline and structure into the information services process.

Another technique, evolving over a period of years, consists of tools and approaches. The tools include the data-flow diagrams, but with very specific symbols. This is used to model functions. The techniques consist of guidelines that are helpful in aiding the information services analysts in going from an idea to a design concept and eventually a well-organized system model. The technique addresses the issue of system size and uses a technique called *event partitioning* to identify levels and systems boundaries. This allows the analyst to correlate user events to their corresponding system partitions or sectors. It always adheres to several important principles:

1. Modeling is good as a useful and educational activity; it should cover three dimensions: function, data, and time and control.
2. Alteration is good, so the analyst should review, change, review, and improve on a continuing basis.
3. Partitioning is good, as subsystems are more easily handled than the whole behemoth.

A fourth technique from the premier software engineers is a variation of the entity-relationship approach. This approach addresses the shortcoming of most approaches, which is their isolated views of a system. Most systems of mission-critical proportions are integrated subsystems, so purchasing is integrated with accounts payable, order entry is integrated with accounts receivable, and all financial modules are integrated with general ledger. This entity-relational approach is an approach that relates apparently disparate subsystems and user requirements to specific databases. This approach has consistently been the most popular method for data modeling and database design. The definitions of entity and relationship are key to the success and to the *understanding* of this approach. An *entity* is a thing, a concept, an organization, or an event occurring in the organization doing the modeling. An *entity type* is a classification of entities, and *relationship* is an interaction between entities. A *relationship type* is a group or cluster of relationships based on certain criteria. In this, the next step is to identify the relationship types, which means the relationship of the relationship types. Next, the analyst should identify the attributes of each entity-relationship and express these in graphs as circles or ellipses. Finally, the entire entity-relationship is converted into conventional file and database structures.

The fifth technique to be briefly reviewed here is the structure–design approach, which originated in the 1960s, beginning with data-flow diagrams, called *bubble charts*. This approach includes system-structure modeling to put each component and module of the system into one compact model. This overview, which was first introduced by the designer in the 1960s, is an excellent way to put systems into perspective, followed by an analysis of complexity referred to as *coupling and cohesion*.

This overall structure–design method consists of five steps as follows:

1. Define the systems requirements around a data-flow diagram.
2. Select an appropriate software organizational model based upon the structure of the problem.
3. Decompose overall functions into subfunctions and compose primitive functions into higher-level functions to meet the requirements.
4. Use various design rules and measures to refine the design.
5. Complete detailed design for all modules.

So five systems engineers have developed approaches and techniques that are all designed to assist the information services analysts in their definition and translation of user requirements into workable systems. It is, of course, another complication leading to the difficulties in system analysis and, therefore, in development of in-house systems. One software engineer observed that these different approaches reflect some real technical differences, but more than anything else, competing approaches are based on product differentiation and personal egos. Maybe so, but this does not make the information services analyst's job any easier and does not address his or her need to implement the recommendations of the business process re-engineering team. Yet if we do not implement, the team has simply developed a new document for the shelf.

SCARCITY AND MISUSE OF TALENT

There is not an unlimited supply of good information services analysts. Look at any metropolitan newspaper, and you will see numerous job openings for information services analysts, programmer analysts, and other generic job titles. We all know that there are a plethora of search firms that specialize in recruiting data processing personnel. Now there are job fairs and open houses in which the employers share a time and location to interview information services experts. There is not an unlimited supply of people to develop systems in-house, which also contributed to the swing from in-house development to packaged software.

Another complicating factor, of course, is that many information services analysts do not understand the business application that they must re-engineer for the user. Why should they? The analysts typically have not worked the problem, or had hands-on experience with the business process they are being asked to re-engineer to implement a new solution. This has been a problem since the inception of automation, and it is a real and concrete reason why many users opted for packaged solutions in the last generation and will look at them for re-engineered solutions. The software salesmen knew their products and applications. We have always been impressed with IBM's industry specialists. Nevermind that you did not see them after the sale; they knew their industry and their product. The same cannot often be said for the in-house information services analyst.

The answer is not to throw more people at the problem either. Computer Associate's Chairman, Charles Wang, addressed that issue. According to Wang, a project team should never exceed six analysts. When there are more, the project should be broken down into small segments and the team kept under six. When the first schedule is missed, two analysts are removed, leaving the team at four. The next missed schedule results in a team of two; the next results in one analyst remaining. Wang postulates that the remaining analyst is probably doing all the work anyway. If another schedule is missed, so is that analyst. Quite frankly, I do not know where Wang goes from there, but I know he is correct. Computer Associates is a multibillion-dollar corporation; that is proof positive.

The answer to the uninformed information services analyst is not, therefore, to add more analysts. The answer is to provide a better means for re-engineers to communicate re-engineering recommendations to the information services analysts, a better means than any that has existed until now. For without some better means, the problems of implementing re-engineering recommendations will remain, and the stumbling block that caused users to live with obsolete systems will not be addressed. The good news is that tools are available to save the day in-house.

LACK OF DEVELOPMENT TOOLS

Most analysts do not use any tools other than pencil and paper—and please do not tell us that most analysts use CASE tools. According to Case Research Corporation of Bellevue, Washington, fewer than 10 percent of potential customers of CASE tools are even dabbling in it. One New York bank spent over $500,000 with a single CASE developer and does not use a single copy of the systems engineering tools. The reasons for this will be explored in a later chapter.

So the analysts use pencil and paper. They draft documents in response to a re-engineered recommendation and present their recommendations to users. It is simply too difficult to make changes to this draft, and we used white-out on our standard specifications, but the original soon became tattered. The iterative process of ever-changing requirements is not conducive to pencil and paper. Or is it the other way around?

Information services analysts need tools if there is going to be a good way to implement new business processes for mission-critical applications. CASE tools have been around for almost ten years yet only 10 percent of users are even dabbling with them. CASE tools are supported by national conferences (e.g., CASECON), seminars and courses (e.g., Digital Corporation), and training by the vendors (e.g., Knowledgeware). Yet analysts are not using them, and the potential for implementing re-engineered business processes may well suffer. The bookshelves will be cluttered with good ideas, or implementation efforts will be scrapped when faced with the high cost of consultants when they bid to implement recommendations.

There appears to be five serious obstacles to overcome before we can feasibly and effectively implement re-engineered processes. These are as follows:

- A failure in communications between the information services analyst and users of business processes.
- Changing conditions in business process requirements and a lack of capabilities to react economically to these changes.
- Confusing approaches recommended by software engineers as solutions to process design.
- Scarcity of talent to define and implement new business processes.
- Lack of tools which information services can use successfully.

A new approach seems needed and we are poised to embrace it. It is referred to as Ways of Working.

WAYS OF WORKING

Ways of Working is a basis or foundation upon which design can comfortably rest. It is a recognized need and a methodology. To paraphrase one expert, companies' systems and methods are still locked in computers. What is needed is a framework for using tools in new and appropriate ways. Without a new approach to Ways of Working, all the CASE tools, standard development methodologies, and other new-age methodologies will have no impact.

We, together, must explore the framework for using new implementation engineering tools and understand and adopt a new approach to design and implementation of re-engineered business processes, or they simply will not be implemented.

8

The Requirements for
Implementation Engineering

Just as we see what is needed, we see why what was available was not appropriate. CASE tools would seem to be a viable alternative for use in documenting processes for re-engineering. CASE tools are programmed automation of the various techniques (e.g., data-flow diagrams) discussed in previous chapters. These tools are used for documentation of new systems. Can they also be used to define user requirements for re-engineered systems?

The question arises as to the extent to which CASE tools are being used in re-engineering studies and the follow-up implementation projects. According to Case Research Corporation, fewer than 10 percent of customers (computer users) are even dabbling in CASE technology. The same results were noted in a study of over 3,000 information services executives. The survey covered the United States, Japan, Australia, France, and the United Kingdom. The results indicated the following:

- Only 20 percent of data processing installations worldwide are using CASE technology.
- Seven percent of the installations have tried CASE technology and *rejected* it.
- Thirty percent of the respondents to the study felt that the main problem to CASE was cutting through the hype of unsubstantiated claims for the products by the vendors.

It is difficult to analyze which of these results is the most shocking. Only 20 percent of all installations are even using CASE technology; 7 percent tried and rejected it; 30 percent think the products cannot substantiate the salesmen's claims. Each is a poor statement of findings in itself.

Another finding from the same study deserves attention. As we pointed out earlier, CASE tools may be divided into three distinct categories. There is the upper CASE product, used for design and modeling of systems; there is the lower CASE product, used to generate code; and there is the integrated product, which is a complete product of upper and lower CASE products. The study showed that in the United States only 23 percent of respondents are using upper CASE tools and 21 percent are using lower CASE tools. In both instances, almost 50 percent of the companies responding have not yet considered using CASE tools.

The Japanese offer an interesting story in regard to the status of CASE tools. In Japan, only 9 percent of the respondents are using upper CASE, while 21 percent are using lower CASE tools. This is interesting in that the lower CASE tools, which generate code, are generally considered to be the productivity enhancers; more so than the upper CASE tools. In the upper CASE product, the claims are more in the direction of better design, fewer errors, and more comprehensive systems, rather than more productivity.

The CASE vendors remain optimistic about their markets because they are concentrating on the number of users who plan to use CASE technology. In the United States, 25 percent plan to use upper CASE tools, and 21 percent plan to use lower CASE tools, while 32 percent plan to use CASE tools when (and if) sufficiently integrated. The optimism is probably ill-founded, as the study does not indicate in what time frame they are considering using them. In addition, almost one-half the users apparently have not yet explored CASE.

Another disturbing trend in Japan is the percentage of responding users that have rejected CASE tools; 17 percent have rejected upper CASE and 16 percent have rejected lower CASE. This can only be reasonably explained as disappointment in not achieving the benefits anticipated or promised. We will explore the reality of the CASE world shortly, but offer the opinion here that the Japanese experience is very understandable based on our experience. It may well take longer to develop systems and complete the systems design using CASE tools.

Using CASE is an important concept to understand as well. There are wide variations in the term *using*; that is, what does using mean? One research project on CASE maintains a database resulting in the data shown in Table 8.1.

Of the many interesting findings about CASE, we found the analysis of users of CASE to be particularly informative. It revealed the following: Very few users have a department-wide commitment to CASE tools (21.0%), and even fewer have a corporate-wide commitment (11.2%). The use of CASE tools, then, is experimental. Fully 35 percent of the users are trying CASE in a pilot project mode, as shown in Table 8.2.

The pilot project is common today. The information services department will purchase one copy of a CASE tool, select a small team and a small, usually insignificant project, and give it a try. That probably means that 35 percent, or more than one-third, of those responding positively in the previously mentioned study are not really using CASE effectively yet, but are in pilot project mode.

TABLE 8.1
Worldwide CASE Status (in Percentages)

	Status	Japan	U.K.
Upper CASE	Using Now	9	22
	Plan to Use	20	30
	Rejected	17	5
	Not Yet Considered	54	43
Lower CASE	Using Now	21	27
	Plan to Use	17	27
	Rejected	16	8
	Not Yet Considered	46	38
Integrated	Using Now	3	27
	Plan to Use	12	25
	Rejected	23	8
	Not Yet Considered	62	40

TABLE 8.2
Analysis of CASE Users (in Percentages)

Planned Use Adoption Stage	CASE Use Now	Planned
Pilot Project	35.5	10.3
Departmental	21.0	30.5
Rapid turnaround	14.2	19.4
Quality improvement	14.1	12.9
Corporate-wide	11.2	21.9
Involve end-users	4.1	5.1

Another observation concerns involvement of users. It has been touted all along that the CASE tools would be the means to communicate with the end-users. Earlier, we observed that the graphics capabilities of CASE tools and methods could potentially facilitate communications. In the study, users reporting indicate only 4.1 percent involve end-users and only 5.1 percent plan to involve them. This is not a valid use of CASE tools as we interpret the response.

Another indication of lack of use of CASE products comes to us directly from a user. A well-known consultant was contacted by large banks in the northeast. In the first instance, the consultant met with two vice presidents of information services and four key analysts. At that meeting, the consultant demonstrated the use of graphics to define systems requirements and begin the business process re-engineering study. This bank had been using a loan processing system for over fifteen years and had determined that it was now obsolete and badly in need of re-engineering and of updating the user documentation.

The presentation was well received. Graphics were viewed as a new and nonconventional approach to business re-engineering. The group viewed the demonstration of presenting structure charts and decomposing to lower levels of detail using the mouse. They were impressed with the approach and the capabilities to solve their specific problem. They ultimately rejected the approach as being too unique and revolutionary for the bank at that time. The interesting thing is that this bank had purchased over $100,000 worth of CASE tools from a leading vendor. There are a great number of information services departments who may affirm they have CASE products, but do not, in fact, use them.

In the second instance, the consultants were contacted by another major vendor of CASE tools concerning a banking customer. In this instance, in which the consultant will soon be actively engaged, the bank has purchased over one-hundred copies of a superb CASE tool with integrated functionality. To this date, the bank has not used CASE in other than a small and inconclusive pilot study. The assignment, should the consultant choose to accept it: How should the customer use more than a half-million-dollar investment?

The pilot project approach has given us some cause for concern. It appears to be a ploy to overcome some natural resistance to change. Vendors have been known to suggest that a customer purchase their products, form a small pilot group, select a pilot project which is not in the mainstream, and test the capabilities of CASE. Aside from our belief that this is a poor sales technique, the approach is, most often, not successful. CASE is a long-term, corporate-wide approach. There is almost no way to set up a perfect test in which two like teams undertake a like project, under like conditions. What information services department is going to allocate its scarce resources to duplicate projects to prove the validity of the claim that CASE increased productivity?

Of course, there is quite a significant learning curve anyway. A pilot project suffers in this regard. In conclusion, we may see studies showing 10 to 25 percent of information services departments using CASE, but it is a real question as to the degree to which this is so. Some consulting firms use CASE in their business process re-engineering practice, but most do not.

WHY INFORMATION SERVICES IS NOT USING CASE

There are a number of reasons why CASE tools have not reached their full potential and should not be used in business process re-engineering projects. Three primary categories of reasons are (1) existing barriers, (2) time commitments, and (3) lack of agreement on structured methodologies. Each will be discussed in this chapter.

Existing Barriers

There are generally four barriers to success cited by respondents to an earlier study. They are listed in Table 8.3. Cutting through the hype is ranked highly. These ostensibly are the promises made by vendors as to the benefits of their products. It is probably justified to some extent in that there are over one-hundred diverse vendors of CASE products.

Each CASE vendor is touting its products, and we see the same features and functions race today in promotions of applications software packages. (We observed this in *Selecting and Installing Software Packages*, Greenwood Press, 1987, by Jud Breslin.) With this many vendors, and more entering the fray every day, there will be attraction and consolidations; both have already begun. It is natural to expect the vendors to promote their products with features, success stories, and claims.

It is this phenomenon that the respondents identified as a major barrier to successful use of CASE. We are a little skeptical of this, however. We wonder if this is not smoke and an excuse to justify a fear of change by many information services respondents. Recently, we attended CASECON, a very good CASE tools conference. During the various presentations, we frequently heard "show me." Cutting through the hype may be more than meets the eye, we are afraid.

We think that justifying the cost, also a high-mark barrier, may be a more legitimate concern to potential users. Some CASE tools are not inexpensive including Knowledgeware, by the company of the same name. More important, the initial cost is not the total cost of using CASE tools. And so the question arises as to how to justify the expense of CASE tools to management. The problem in justification is to quantify the benefits, which are, at best, difficult. For example:

- *Requirements*: CASE tools may assist in better development of user requirements. How can this be quantified in terms of dollars, man hours, user satisfaction, and so forth?

TABLE 8.3
Ranking of Barriers to Success (Using CASE Products)

Barrier	Asia	Europe	U.S.
Assessing Products	2nd	3rd	2nd
Implementation	3rd		
Justifying the Cost	1st	2nd	
Cutting through the Hype	1st	2nd	1st

- *Error reduction*: CASE tools allow use of a structured approach to design. How can this be quantified until the project ends and the system is operative, if at all?
- *Maintenance*: Systems developed using CASE technologies require less maintenance. Again, how is this to be quantified as a justification?
- *User involvement*: We have seen that CASE tools do not automatically assure user involvement, and to our knowledge, there are no precise measures of the economic benefits to user involvement anyway (although we know its benefits).

There is substance here. We believe that cost justification is a real barrier to successful use of CASE tools. CASE tools are designed to improve communication, improve systems design and effectiveness, and increase systems and programming productivity. How do information services professionals prove their case?

Choosing and assessing products is a major concern for our European and Japanese information services counterparts. Although not ranked in the top three concerns in the United States, we must know that this is an issue here as well. With more than one-hundred vendors offering combinations of upper, lower, and integrated products, it must be difficult to select a product to be the standard for a department. In addition, it is questionable whether one CASE product is best for re-engineering. That, in part, has caused the product and vendor glut that we see today.

There are many factors involved in the decision, too. Unlike the software packages industry, which is reaching a high degree of maturity and where comparative methodologies are available, the newly formed CASE industry does not now have a foolproof comparative study or technique. Some of the factors that must be considered in evaluating CASE products are as follows:

- Engineering techniques (DFD, structure charts, entity-relationship diagrams, etc.).
- Ease of use (a critical factor).
- Ability to decompose (some products are limited here).
- Data dictionary capabilities (and flexibility).
- Integration of functions (upper and lower case).
- Vendor stability (essential element in the evaluation).
- Price (all over the map).
- Expandability (to new techniques if they become necessary).
- Documentation (and training support).
- Bug-free (a difficult factor to evaluate).

The problem of having to adopt to methods and standards seems to be a unique problem for the independent Americans. This is the problem that is more than a mere barrier to using a tool; it is a mind-set that will not easily be overcome.

Time Commitments

Another reason that information services departments have not overwhelmingly endorsed CASE tools for re-engineering is the time factor. In the overall time frame of the systems development life cycle, it may be shown that CASE reduces the time to complete a project. This is especially true if lower case code generation is included in the time frame. But, without a reasonable doubt, designing systems from inception with a CASE tool takes longer than the same design effort without a CASE tool—*even after the learning curve.*

Experience proves it; no honest vendor will deny it. It takes longer to develop data-flow diagrams, entity-relational diagrams, and structure charts than it does to lay out a system Ways of Working format with narrative, flow charts, screen designs, and reports. The CASE approach is time consuming and is not the best approach, unfortunately.

The problem is: Can the overworked, behind schedule, information services department with a mountain of maintenance agree to a more time-consuming approach to systems design? Will management acquiesce to a new approach that is costly, requires a long burn-in period, and initially prolongs development of re-engineered systems? The answer to both of these questions, in many instances, is no. Management undertakes a lengthy re-engineering analysis, and is not prone to take two years to execute it.

Agreement on Structured Methodology

Finally, the issue of standards simply exacerbates the whole issue. There is a hesitancy on the part of many to adopt structured analysis in the first place and a specific modeling convention in the second place. The president of a large CASE vendor expressed the concern that the "cream had been skimmed," and now the hard-sell must begin. The cream, simply put, are those large information services departments that have adapted structured analysis as the standard approach to systems design. For them, the decision is easy because the CASE tools will only make the process more efficient and more effective, as we have already discussed. But what about the remaining 80 percent of users? They must walk first and adopt structured analysis before they will adopt CASE.

Another president of a CASE vendor recently told us at a convention that the average information services employee does not understand structured analysis. "We start now with education on structured methods, and then, hopefully, get time to discuss our product," he told us.

We think the proliferation of technique just complicates the issue. There are different techniques, and each has a different touch or feel. For example, there is no standard for data-flow diagrams:

• One software engineer uses one icon for processes and straight arrows for flows.

- A second software engineer recommends bubbles and curved arcs to represent the same thing.

There is no standard as to which techniques should be employed to define systems. We observed one young CASE engineer fill a complete blackboard with products that she recommended; they included, as well as I can remember, the following:

- Data-flow diagrams.
- Entity-relational diagrams.
- State-transition diagrams (time-phased presentation).
- CRUD chart (create, report, update, and display).
- Various models and prototypes.

This analyst is still working on defining an elementary system that will never fly.

This lack of standards simply causes indecision and uncertainty in the information services world. To us, it is both real and understandable. CASE tools are valuable tools; structured analysis only makes sense; but they are not working now. Something else is needed for use in the initial re-engineering study and the eventual implementation of the recommended new business process.

WAYS OF WORKING

Defining our Ways of Working, on the other hand, is a standard. It draws on existing standards including Windows, UNIX, and software products off-the-shelf. It is patented.

9

The New Approach

Only five years ago, the search began for a new approach. It all started at the international consulting organization in the business of evaluating, recommending, and implementing applications software packages. It was only too clear that we were reinventing the wheel on each engagement. We were re-engineering poorly, as described in previous chapters. We unsuccessfully employed the old systems life cycle for recommendation and implementation, whether for in-house development or package selection. As such, we defined the client's information requirements, designed a list of these requirements, compared this list with available packages, did a detailed design of modifications to the selected package or to a new in-house system, and so on.

It is clear that we were learning little from the past. We continued, in many instances and with many consulting firms, to underutilize computing power and resort to pencil and pen. This redundancy and duplication of effort cried for a new approach to re-engineering, systems design, and the systems development life cycle.

The pace of advancement in technology reflects the problem we face in trying to improve system effectiveness.

Pace of Advancement, 1981–1994

Factor	Pace of Advancement
Computer hardware	Fast
Computer software	Medium-Fast
Development methodology	Slow
Information services management	Slow

When thinking of how to deal with the problems of methodology and unchanging information services management, four potential solutions surface: (1) change or restructure information services management, (2) experiment with new development capabilities and new methods, (3) transfer more responsibility to end-users (empowerment), and (4) use information services consultants with the appropriate industry experience and requisite technical skills. The latter is better known now as part of the systems integration approach.

We embraced these four potential solutions and added a summary footnote. What is really needed, we concluded, is to improve the ability of users and corporate management to review and decide together what they want and to understand and control adequately what they are getting. With these precepts in mind, we justified our search for a new approach to business process improvement and systems development.

Under the title *Innovation*, a major U.S. aerospace and defense company put the data processing industry and its past into perspective. Comparing the industry to the fabled tower of Babel, Lockheed observed that the parable is older than writing itself, coming to us from the first murmuring of civilization. Yet its lesson seems to have been aimed specifically at the late twentieth century.

In Genesis 11, we read of an unnamed people building a great city on the plain of Shinar (Mesopotamia). To the narrator of this parable, peering across time and desert from his own nomadic traditions, these folk were awesomely clever. They spoke a common language, and therefore, nothing was impossible to them.

The plan of these ingenious people was to erect a huge temple tower, whose top would reach into heaven. It was to be an altar to their own intellect and would be called Babel, or "Gate of God." But God himself came down and walked the streets of their city and saw their project under construction. The hubris of this arrogant race angered him. He passed his hand over the city and cursed it. Now where there had been one language were suddenly hundreds. Confusion reigned. Nothing was possible. The people abandoned their city and scattered across the land, taking with them their bewildering tongues. And their vaunted temple, the tower of Babel, was left untopped; carrion for the wind.

The lesson taught by this ancient parable is uncannily prescient for us in the twentieth century. The revolution in information technology during the past four decades has brought with it the ancient curse of Babel. Every decade witnesses the birth of new computer companies, all fiercely competing with faster, more powerful hardware, new formats, and new languages. All contribute to an atmosphere of discord that the narrator of the Biblical story would have no trouble recognizing, despite the great gulf of time.

Lockheed goes on to say that it has recognized the discord and finds the solution to be "open systems." This means synthesizing apparently incompatible systems, thus working against the Babel effect. If everyone once again speaks the same language, Lockheed concludes, who knows what wonders are possible? That must be UNIX.

Lockheed is right on target. It is their contention that the ills of data processing with poor execution, inadequate solutions to management's information needs, and poor utilization of amazing capabilities of the computer and the information services staff, still is almost entirely due to a lack of communications. That is the communications, as Lockheed points out, between computer companies and computer users and the communications between information services professionals, re-engineers, and the ultimate user community. We concur with Lockheed for attacking the former with systems integration; we complement this approach by attacking the latter: communication between users, re-engineers, and data processors. Once again, we return to our four target areas for potential breakthrough and improvement:

1. Changing and restructuring information services roles and responsibilities.
2. Incorporating new methodologies and a new approach, specifically a new systems development life cycle.
3. Transferring more responsibility to users for the success of design and implementation of *their* systems (empowerment).
4. Adopting systems integration concepts.

We believe that the critical beginning point for a new approach and strategy is a comprehensive method—Ways of Working—which comprises the tools available to information services and the analysts. We turned initially to simple graphics tools and evaluated these tools as a starting point for a new strategy. After several years of usage, we have some indications of the factors that vendors maintain will influence both productivity improvements and the quality of the final systems development. They are shown in Table 9.1. These are two important considerations, of course, in recommending graphics as an integral part of a new strategy. This survey of one-hundred organizations that use graphics portions of CASE tools was revealing. One question asked was the extent to which improvements were attained in seven critical areas. The survey is interesting in what it shows. Results are summarized in Table 9.2.

Communications between users and the information services staff was significantly improved using graphics tools. This is because information services now has a means to converse (in graphics) that is better than long narrative dialogues. This, we conclude, is a very positive step in recommending a new approach to systems development, and quite frankly, is justification in itself for using graphics technology. The graphics tools also improve communications through the displays of tables and screens to which a user can easily relate. In addition, the ability to discuss changes and make them easily probably contributed to the high ranking of communications between users and information services.

Another encouraging, but probably anticipated, result was a marked improvement in productivity and system development with improvements in documentation. Documentation, as we pointed out previously, has always been a problem child in the systems development process—the necessary evil that is always put off until the bitter end. This is because it is not very exciting and is a laborious, time-consuming task. The nice thing about graphics tools is that, if properly used, much of the documentation (including screens, logic, and data) is

TABLE 9.1
Factors That Influence Productivity and Quality Improvements
(in Percentages)

	Extent of Improvement		
Factor of Improvement	Significantly	Moderately	Not at All
1. Communications (User/MIS)	53	47	0
2. Communications (Within MIS)	20	67	13
3. Documentation	67	33	0
4. Project control	20	20	60
5. Project standards	20	40	40
6. Management visibility	0	60	40
7. Project consistency	20	60	20

accomplished during the design phase of the old systems development life cycle. This capability is reflected in the survey in which 67 percent of the respondents reported a significant improvement using graphics technology.

The survey further indicated that over 50 percent of respondents believe that there are significant to moderate improvements in setting and maintaining project standards and consistency among projects. Management visibility was not improved significantly, but there was a majority feeling that management visibility had been improved moderately. Project control was not effected much, and 40 percent of the respondents found no improvement at all in the areas of project standards and management visibility. As a result, we should look closely at how graphics tools are interfaced with project management software (if at all), and how these tools are impacting standards and are presented to management. We consider this a favorable analysis, and at the same time, an opportunity to improve how graphics tools are used in the systems development life cycle and implementation of re-engineered business processes.

A second question in this survey is also important in our thesis for improved re-engineering and systems development. This has to do with the impact of the use of graphics tools on the development effort itself.

Do not underestimate the impact of "more enjoyable," as this could easily improve productivity. The results here are important in evaluating the use of graphics in improving systems development, in that changes are deemed to be facilitated with graphics. We observed earlier that it was imperative that users be able to review and change designs as conditions change and better solutions arise. We warned against "freezing" the design, and here we see an opportunity to use an interactive process in reviewing, approving, and improving systems design.

In addition, the information services analysts with graphics tools will perform their design more thoroughly before launching into programming. This is yet another positive note. In fact, other than speculation on maintenance, this was

TABLE 9.2
Impact of Use of Graphics Tools on the System's Development
(in Percentages)

	Change Realized	
Type of Change	*Yes*	*No*
1. Ability to make more changes	67	33
2. More likely to design before programming	80	20
3. Likelihood of easier maintenance	40	60
4. Ease of graphical representation	93	7
5. More enjoyable	93	7

indeed a positive look at how information services analysts can use graphics technology. Clearly, the capability to develop graphics representations more easily will improve communications, leading to better quality systems.

It is a matter of drawing on the strengths of graphics tools, integrating them better into the systems development life cycle, and overcoming some of the resistance to change that we have previously noted. We believe that the focus on graphics tools will not be skewed too far toward productivity and that the real issue may be quality of the information systems being developed. We believe that productivity will be improved in the long run. It may be in the short run as well. We also believe that the new graphics tools are cost effective, in the short and in the long run. It may be in the short run but it is difficult to prove now in either long or short term.

So will more information services departments implement graphics? A survey of 154 top information services executives verifies the tone we have tried to describe. This survey, summarized in Table 9.3, showed cost is still a major issue to these top executives.

Implementation and acceptance, even with the benefits we have seen, will not be easy. There must be a structure for it. One successful user of graphics is a subsidiary of a major automotive company. There, one vice president praised his experience with graphics, yet he warned that if you drop a new tool in a typical chaotic information services environment, you will not get much out of it, and it will become shelfware. If, however, you combine graphics with heavy emphasis on structural design and process improvements and small teams, you may get positive results.

If properly incorporated, then, we may succeed with graphics. This corresponds to our earlier observations: Without a new approach to systems architecture, all the tools, systems development methodologies, and other new-age methodologies will not make a difference.

We believe this is true and accounts, in our opinion, for the lack of success to date in effectively implementing new business processes. Therefore, the need for a better solution was justified in our minds and in those of our colleagues.

TABLE 9.3
Primary Obstacles to Implementing Graphics (in Percentages)

Issue	Agree (%)
1. Tools are too expensive	60.5
2. Benefits not yet demonstrated	50.6
3. Too many tools and too few standards	38.8
4. Developer resistance	25.0
5. Shortage of networks	19.7
6. Training too expensive	18.4

WAYS OF WORKING ADDRESSES THESE ISSUES

A Ways of Working approach addresses the problems that have plagued information services for so long. First, relative to changes in structure and approach, management should adopt a strategy of information systems repository. The trend toward data repositories and data warehouses should include a systems process and procedures repository. The logic is overwhelming for such a repository in a retrievable format. Enormous efficiencies accrue from defining how we do things and maintaining that information in a single location. This emphasis on documentation of our business processes will be necessary to elevate the chief information officer and the information services discipline to the key management structure required by this competitive business environment.

Why has this not been done before? One reason is the understandable technological bent of information services. Another is the hardware manufacturers who inundate us with quicker, slicker, and trickier hardware at a time when we do not know how to use what we have very well. Another reason is that literally no one today has a repository of business processes and procedures. But in the final analysis, there has been no real interest or any usable methodology for accomplishing a meaningful and usable procedural repository like Ways of Working. That such capability now exists means a restructuring of approach of the information services discipline is indeed possible and required. This is so for all of the reasons explored, including reduction of unnecessary and redundant consulting fees, improved business processes, and multiple views of our Ways of Working.

Second, in relation to the need for new approaches and new methods, these new implementation engineering tools provide just that. The Ways of Working methodology facilitates a repository of graphic-oriented business processes supported by detailed work statements (procedures), which are also graphics (narrative depictions of how we do things). This is no CASE mentality, but a user understandable template of major business processes. And because it is user understandable, it facilitates our third requirement to advance systems and motivate the information services function.

Third, in regard to transferring more responsibility to the user community, the new implementation engineering tools are based on more visibility of business processes. Clearly, the Ways of Working concept dictates that we define, in graphics, our processes and procedures and store them in a retrievable repository that is easily retrieved and easily modified. Because we are not using methodologies only known to technicians, users can be brought into the fray and participate in defining, improving, and managing the thing they know best—their own processes and procedures.

According to the Standish Group International, a market research firm in Dennis, Massachusetts, cited in a November, 1996 issue of *Computerworld*, a survey of more than 300 information services executives reported that the lack of user involvement is the chief reason that systems implementation projects fail. Lack of user involvement, according to the survey, ranked even higher than a lack of management support or a lack of clear project and business objectives. Think of it: The same problem exists that existed two decades ago—a clear lack of user involvement.

The primary cause of this malfunction, according to Standish Group management, is just what we said: the lack of communications. Information services has created its own language, reveled in the mystique, and employed the obtuse methodologies inherent in CASE tools. The users, some observe, are the victims of this communications void. There are several ways to get the user involved, reports the Standish Group:

1. *Identify the Correct User*
   - Clearly identify the user base (everyone who will use the application) through extensive interviews, and select someone who emulates these opinions.
   - Structure this process in stages to gain constant feedback from all users.
   - Structure a plan for gaining customer input, not just internal user input.

2. *Involve the User Early and Often*
   - Get the user to commit to ownership of the project for its entire life cycle, including development, implementation, and maintenance.
   - Motivate the user through roles and incentives.
   - Educate and negotiate with the user regarding the roles and responsibilities of ownership. Listen to the users' expectations. What does "involvement" mean to them?
   - Assign a facilitator or liaison.

3. *Create and Maintain a Quality Relationship*
   - Lay the ground rules for effective teamwork.
   - Make an effort to understand the users' business.
   - Define a method for managing your expectations of one another (may include creating contracts and written rules).
   - Hold regular progress meetings involving the user.

- Publish quality metrics to measure progress.

4. *Make Improvement Easy*
   - Learn the users' language.
   - Proactively solicit the users' opinions.
   - Show the user that his or her opinions make a difference.
   - Make sure there's a demonstrated benefit for user involvement. (The Standish Group International, Dennis, Massachusetts, 1996.)

Using the Ways of Working approach accomplishes the major requirements here. It structures the process in stages or clusters, business processes, and procedures. It encourages user commitment in the definition of how we work. It fosters understanding of the user's business. It encourages progress sessions in a joint application development environment. It can be related to metrics, as in the AMR Supply Chain Model discussed earlier.

The clearest indication that Ways of Working is the appropriate concept, however, is the issue of making improvements to systems easier than in the past. The users language is in sync with the technologists in graphics depiction of what we do and how we do it. It allows very proactive or iterative solicitation of users' opinions, views, and knowledge of how things work. Such communication using this documentation methodology obviously and naturally shows the users that their opinions do make a difference and should lead to demonstratable benefits to the enterprise.

Fourth, and finally, Ways of Working provides a clear opportunity to improve systems and get better re-engineering results because it allows enterprises to use consultants and systems integrators effectively and at a reasonable cost. This is because Ways of Working defines, in understandable format, what we know best: how things are done, leaving the systems integrator to recommend and consult. This is only as it should be.

CONCLUSION

We have observed that we have not yet been totally successful in systems implementations and in improving operations through re-engineering. We believe that this is a result of an unchanged information services structure failing to seek new methodologies, failing to empower users, and misusing consultants and systems integrators. One answer to these four dilemmas that will advance systems and foster better re-engineering of business processes is to adopt a methodology that defines clearly, concisely, and understandably how we work and how we do things. Coming from a position of strength, a knowledge of how things work, puts management in the position of controlling work, managing operations, utilizing systems integrators, reducing auditing fees, and obtaining compliance with regulations that are market-driven, as well as often being business necessities. It is all worth it. It is an idea whose time has come and it may even be a management dream come true.

10

Ways of Working: The Requirement

Implementation engineering tools, such as Ways of Working, provide the power and flexibility to model a process (e.g., a business process). Remembering our earlier analysis of these tools, we opined that the implementation engineering tools must possess certain criteria including the following:

- Make business process more visible.
- Assure manageable customization.
- Facilitate modeling and prototyping.
- Incorporated into a repository of processes.

Visibility is assured with graphics presentations of processes decomposing to procedures and inputs and outputs, including screens, forms, and reports. Manageability of customization is attained when the proper software (programmed in C++, JAVA, or similar) is used to create the visual images and presentation. Similarly, a database must be incorporated to maintain the business processes, procedures, and inputs and outputs. The database is also needed to control security, maintain version control, and keep track of users and trainees (on the system) and their performance.

The umbrella software must also provide the capabilities to model alternative processes in a what-if prototyping mode. The Ways of Working approach includes mapping and an activity-based costing facility that allows users to cost these alternative procedures and therefore, make reasonable judgments or suggest new approaches based on the cost impact.

The umbrella software, providing management over the implementation engineering methodology, should support any like software, such as PC-based project management software, spreadsheets, and word processing. The implementation tool should provide such flexibility that designers can incorporate whatever tools exist to help do what the designer wants done; for example, design a system, implement a packaged software application, obtain certification, develop a disaster-recovery plan, or create an auditor's workbench to cut auditing time and fees.

Ways of Working is such a set of software tools and methodology designed to assist consultants, users, and integrators in defining existing and new systems. It encompasses integrated, interactive, components whose files reside in a design dictionary. Although any number of components may be incorporated in the umbrella software tool, four common components are: (1) project planning, (2) process definition, (3) reinforcement (training), and (4) data identification and tracking. In a PC environment, running under Windows, NT, UNIX, or any number of platforms, users can access each component from a menu, such as that illustrated in Figure 10.1.

THE PRODUCT—FOUR INTEGRATED COMPONENTS

As an example of the implementation tool, four integrated components are common.

Project Planning is a planning facility that enables the efficient planning of design and re-engineering projects. It consists of a detailed plan, including tasks, staffing, and timetables, to complete the study. It allows consultants to develop their own tailored, detailed plan.

Business Process Definition, the second component, is an automated presentation of system and procedural flow charts using graphics software. It reduces the time for consultants to define applications and serves as an ongoing guide to analyzing business functions. The flow charts represent the flow of data and processes (with written descriptions) in an operational environment. They provide a top-down, function-by-function view of applications and business processes.

Ways of Working displays the systems clusters, modules, or components within the application or business process as shown in Figure 10.2.

The first level of decomposition is the cluster. The cluster is the highest level of the system. Clusters then decompose to modules. Users may choose to define the module either functionally or organizationally. The tool displays the functions or business processes of the module (in this case, Order Entry and Billing as shown in Figure 10.3), providing users the opportunity to select a graphics flow chart of a specific function or business process, such as Order Processing (Figure 10.4), or select from a menu of underlying procedures. Users may by-pass the detail list and proceed to an overview of the

FIGURE 10.1
Ways of Working

FIGURE 10.2
Ways of Working: Modules/Components

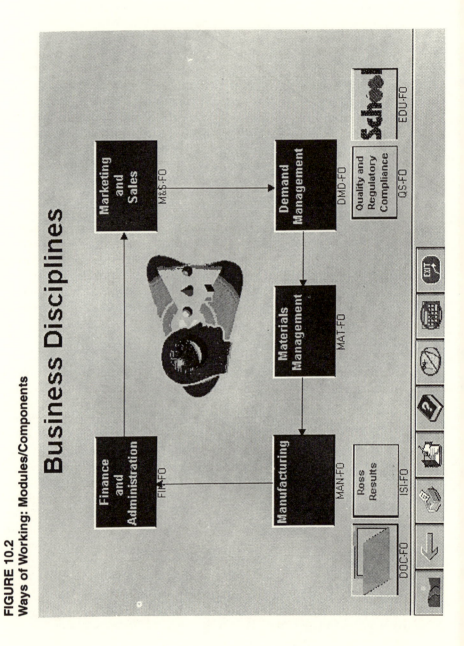

Business Disciplines

FIGURE 10.3
Ways of Working: Functions/Processes

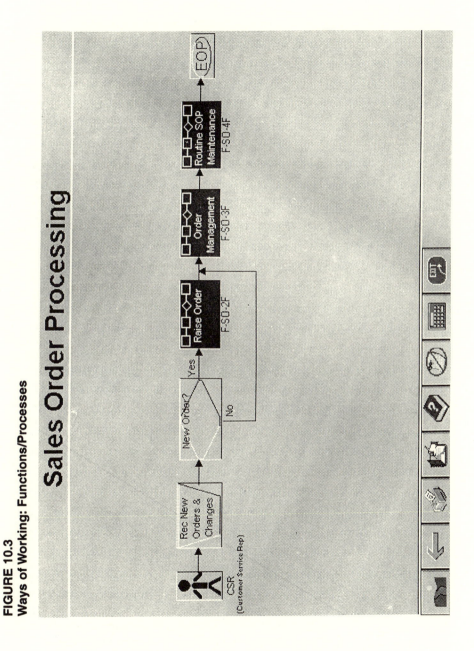

Sales Order Processing

FIGURE 10.4
Ways of Working: Business Process Flow

Sales Order Management

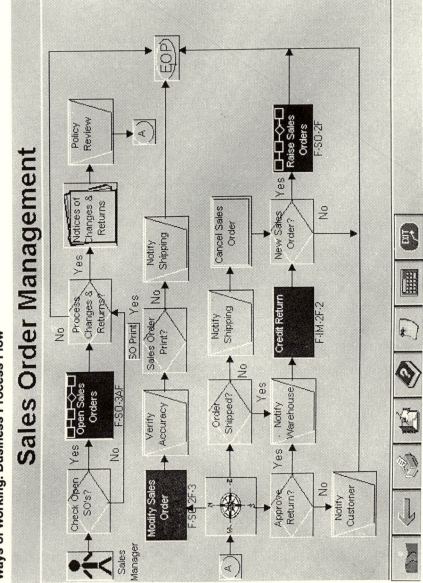

entire module. This overview illustrates how the business processes interrelate. Processes can and do cross modular lines, and the graphic presentation handles this seamlessly. Processes may have subprocesses (a process is a series of work statements or procedures), and the tool seamlessly links icons to subprocesses, next in the chain processes, and more detail procedures: Processes tell users *what* to do and procedures and work statements tell users *how* to do it.

Users may also choose to define modules from an organizational perspective. For users selecting "organization" from the module menu, Ways of Working displays a prototype organization chart identifying all positions required to perform their work with the module (Figure 10.5). From this level in Ways of Working, the user may define specific positions to display the responsibilities for each individual. Organization charts can be accessed from any appropriate level in Ways of Working. The organization at the cluster level usually defines the enterprise; the module defines the department, and the function defines work stations and individual users.

From both organizational and functional perspectives, Ways of Working further explodes to detail procedures, screens, and report layouts. Therefore, the architecture is used to describe exactly how the business process and applications work, explaining underlying procedures, both automated and manual, in increasingly focused steps, ending at the screen and report level. End-users can review the graphics and accompanying narrative to approve and improve procedures, standards, or preferences. Process definition is integrated with the other three components of Ways of Working.

The Business Process Definition uses graphics software, as well, to define and recommend new systems integration opportunities and systems enhancements. It employs the concept of scenarios and it provides users with the opportunity to review the planned changes to the current environment and understand the impact of the recommendations in the same user-friendly way as presented as an environmental definition component. In the architecture, these enhancements and systems integration opportunities can be easily quantified, as we shall soon see.

Reinforcement or Performance Support is a third component of this integrated toolset. Reinforcement is the concept of prompting a user or information services person through the business process in a structural mode, so they can be tested on the process. We are ambivalent on the issue of whether reinforcement should include tests and test scores, but it is clear that such reinforcement should be present. Reinforcement is a critical element in Employee Performance Support Systems (EPSS) of which we have been very supportive.

Ways of Working does not consider reinforcement and process flow charting and definition to be separate entities, exactly. Rather, reinforcement is training on the process environment, which has now been defined to the appropriate level of detail (in fact, may be down to, "press this key and hit the Enter button"). The process environment defines the following:

FIGURE 10.5
Ways of Working: Organization

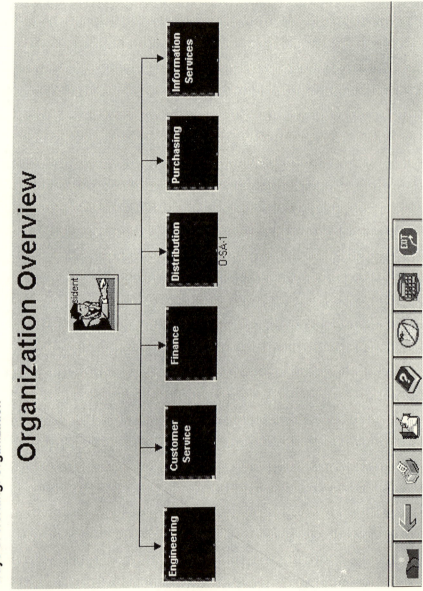

Organization Overview

- What must be done.
- What action triggered it.
- Who must do it.
- What do I do next.
- How do I do it.

Reinforcement does not require redevelopment of a training session or a new curriculum developed by a remote trainer. Reinforcement is a series of prompts (or quizzes) to guide the user through the process. It links to the process. It directly accesses the process—it supports what must be done, by whom, and in what manner. It is classic "Performance Support."

Data Identification and Tracking is a fourth integrated component. As the name implies, it is based on the data used in an application. It is a planning and decision-making facility that simplifies the data elements in spreadsheet format and identifies which procedures and flow charts use the specific data elements. It identifies usage by organization, procedure, and transaction. This component is used to analyze data (including data redundancies, inconsistencies, etc.), assign responsibility for data, analyze the effects of any proposed modifications, and serve as an audit trail in problem resolution. It is used to configure the flow of screens and menus based on setup decisions. It is here that Business Engineering Workbench from SAP excels. Having access to SAP sources, SAP engineers are able to configure the menus on-line, thus vastly reducing the setup time required to implement SAP's R/3 system.

These implementation tools reduce the time, resources, and expense necessary to re-engineer a process through analysis and documentation of business processes. All tasks and responsibilities are identified at the onset in the plan, consultants are guided through procedures with on-line depiction of the Business Process Definition and the Planned Business Process. This creates understanding and concurrence prior to large expenditures. Reinforcement teaches and guides, and Data Tracking is sophisticated and streamlined linking of Data and Business Processes. It all leads to greater *productivity* for users and consultants, a greater *return* on user investment, and a longer *useful* life for proposed systems.

USING THE NEW TOOLS

No two re-engineering studies are exactly the same nor are any two implementation projects. Each is undertaken differently depending on the organization and (1) the resources allocated, (2) the urgency and related timetable, and (3) the sequence of phases, activities, and tasks. There are, however, similarities in the phases of each study.

Recognizing this, the authors designed a project plan as the initial component of its overall re-engineering tool. This planning component, described in the following discussion, is an automated, PC-based project management system, which generically identifies phases, activities, tasks, resources, and dependencies while allowing the engineers to alter each of these as the situation dictates. The process of customizing the plan on-line is referred to as personalization; for example, personalization of the tasks, their dependencies, and the assigned resources.

PLAN: An Integrated Component

The project planning component of Ways of Working is referred to simply as the PLAN. It is a computerized, multiphase compilation of the activities and tasks required to conduct a design study, requirements, definition, or a re-engineering study. It is integrated with three other components of Ways of Working: (1) Business Process Definition and Planned Business Process, (2) Reinforcement, and (3) Data Identification and Tracking. The PLAN is cross referenced to all procedures and transactions graphically displayed in the Environment Definition component. The PLAN also includes all activities and tasks required for developing the planned environment, cost justification, project selection, and conversion planning.

The PLAN addresses the problems inherent in developing a project plan; namely, the identification of tasks, allocation of resources, and setting the sequence and dependencies of the tasks. To address these issues, the PLAN consists of three critical elements. They are

- *Tasks*. The specific tasks within the activities required to conduct the study are set forth in the PLAN.
- *Resources*. Resources are identified at the task level to indicate the organization and job title normally assigned the responsibility for executing the tasks.
- *Dependencies*. The recommended sequence for executing the phases, activities, and tasks is included in the PLAN, and is easily changed by the engineer.

Phases and activities are generic to the planning of all projects. Tasks, resources, and dependencies are input by designers or project leaders to reflect the typical activities of a re-engineering study. The result is a plan which is the basis for estimating the time required to complete the study.

A ten-phase plan is common in products like Computer Associates PowerBench. The phases include the preassessment statement of goals through the postassessment measurement of the study. Each phase is divided into discrete activities required in the study. Phases and activities, therefore, should be developed to assure the correct steps are addressed when beginning or promoting a study.

PLAN: Tasks. Tasks are a finer division of activities for performing a re-engineering study. Resources, in terms of personnel and dependencies, are assigned only to tasks. Engineers may add or delete tasks. For example, tasks would be added for those requirements not normally faced in a typical study. Tasks are also added for unique steps in the study.

PLAN: Resources. Resources assigned to tasks include the generic organization and the job title normally assigned this task (e.g., consultant, MIS analyst, programmer, documentation clerk, etc.). The identification of resources is based on any actual experience performing these studies. Resources are easily added to and deleted from the PLAN. They include not only the generic name, but an estimation of the time to be spent on each task. Engineers may change the time allotments for the plan and each task.

The resources are calculated for a theoretical baseline study. Actual users of the PLAN factor the resource allocations against their project size. The result is a customized allocation of resources to input into the PLAN component of Ways of Working.

PLAN: Dependencies. The PLAN is organized by the recommended sequence of phases, activities, and tasks. This is accomplished by assigning dependencies to each task and organizing phases and activities sequentially. The sequence and dependencies represent experience in conducting these studies. Yet, at the same time, the dependencies and sequence can be easily changed by the engineers to reflect uncommon conditions or some unique realities they face. The assignment of sequence and dependencies is critical to graphically presenting the detailed, customized plan in two distinct formats—Gantt chart and PERT chart. Together, these charts present the overall timetable and the relationship between detailed tasks, activities, and phases.

The PLAN reduces the uncertainty associated with conducting design, requirements, and re-engineering studies. The PLAN allows management to review a preliminary plan, developed by a project leader and personalized by the project team, to clearly see the time required to complete the study. The timetable may be viewed in three levels of detail, in Gantt or PERT formats: by phases, by activities, or by detailed tasks.

Management may tailor the plan to match its overall strategic goals. Using the flexibility of the PLAN, customers may change priorities and add or delete resources. In addition, management may "deadline" schedule the entire project, selecting the completion date, and allowing the PLAN to automatically reschedule tasks and resources to meet the target date.

Once the preliminary schedule has been finalized, reporting of actual performance by tasks is possible, and therefore, management may review the final plan and ongoing progress by phases, activities, and detailed tasks.

These are several ways that the PLAN eliminates the uncertainty. The PLAN allows the project team to present an accurate picture of the time and resources required to complete the study; it allows easy adjustment to changing conditions; and it provides the mechanism to keep the team and management appraised of status, shortfalls, and opportunities to speed up the implementation of recommendations.

The PLAN, furthermore, saves time and reduces the cost of planning the project. The project manager, no longer starting with a blank sheet of paper, is required only to review the list of tasks, add or change resource allocations, and evaluate dependencies. The result is a personalized project plan that reflects actual experiences in similar studies, tempered by the users' own constraints, goals, and resources. PLAN is a very powerful component of an integrated implementation engineering toolset.

Business Process Definition

Documentation of business processes and applications is normally in the form of reports and manuals, which have several distinct disadvantages. The documentation is static and inflexible. Users look at systems differently. Static documentation is not easily changed to reflect the misunderstandings or the different ways the system is used. Frequently, the documentation is not used at all, or is rewritten at significant expense.

The orientation and organization of re-engineering documentation is a second disadvantage. Typically, this documentation is a collection of screens and transactions. They are organized by numerical sequence or by category of transaction, such as inquiries, file maintenance, and batch reporting. The overall approach to documentation begins with a system description of the modules, followed by system functions and features, and ending with the transactions.

This approach does not indicate how the system is actually working, either generically or in a specific environment. It also ignores the organizational implications of who is responsible for performing each function and how the new system will be integrated into the current workflow.

The authors believe systems documentation of this type is inadequate. Proper documentation should present the flow of information and processes in context, by function and organization. Documentation should also include descriptions of all procedures, presented in a flexible format and easily changed to reflect how the procedure will be handled in any specific situation. Finally, thorough user documentation should include screens and transactions directly linked to their use, not by number or category.

Business Process Definition is one of four components of a recommended implementation toolset. Its purpose is to provide a powerful and flexible means to document current systems and procedures as a basic step in re-engineering studies, design studies, and requirements definitions.

Business Process Definition is the automated presentation of systems using sophisticated graphics software. It contains graphics files, which are the process flows and procedures. It includes integrated text files to describe each process and related workflows. Both files can be easily changed by engineers to correct misunderstandings, reflect new data, and address the needs of multidivision companies where the same system is used differently with the various departments. It is also a vehicle to convey procedures and transactions. By doing so, this component overcomes the obstacles of inflexibility and inadequate orientation and organization prevalent in today's static, paper-oriented documentation.

The Business Process Definition flexibility of the component is further enhanced, since each graphical flow and narrative can be printed and distributed to the system's many users. It becomes the basis for verification and confirmation. It is used to document manual procedures and their interfaces with computerized systems.

Business Process Definition is oriented to the functions that must be performed in the day-to-day operations of systems. It is organized by the jobs and human resources required to operate an application. It is presented in multiple levels of detail (see Figures 5.1 through 5.3). At the highest level, applications are organized by clusters. Thereafter, this component decomposes down to screens and transactions. The migration path is:

- *Level 1—Modules.* Identifies and graphically displays the various modules of a system, allowing users availability of two primary means to access detail procedures, for example, by function and organization.

- *Level 2—Process.* Presents the process for each function in the system with detailed, step-by-step flow charts of the tasks to be performed. Presents a generic organization chart for each module. Includes detailed job descriptions for each position having tasks to perform with the system.

- *Level 3—Procedures.* Defines the steps that must be taken to use each feature of the system. Includes system sign-on, accessing the correct screens, input of required and optional data, editing the data, and updating files. Descriptions guide the user from the beginning of a procedure to the end.

- *Level 4—Screens and Transactions.* Presents all screens and transactions used in the system. Describes the use of command keys and function keys, if required. There is a clear and easily illustrated migration path from the initial screen (program ID) through to the screens, forms, and reports.

The key ingredients in this architectural component are flexibility and orientation. Each level, from menu to screens, can be easily modified. Procedures, screens, and transactions can be accessed from any logical point. Icons of each level can be defined to uniquely fit the users identity, preferences, and aesthetics.

Contrasted with the typical manual documentation that results from a reengineering study, this methodology is organized by the functions to be executed and the personnel assigned to perform the tasks. Flow charts at Level 2 display the steps to be completed. Each step decomposes to detail procedures that must be followed in working with the system. In addition, all screens and transactions can be linked directly to the procedures, presenting the engineer with a total picture of the system. Each icon is programmed to decompose to its logical detail:

- Procedural icons decompose to work statements.
- Process icons decompose to subprocesses.
- Decision icons decompose to decision trees.
- Organization icons decompose to job descriptions, and so forth.

The concept encourages documentation of the processes that must be performed. The processes are represented by flow charts of the steps, in sequence. These steps must be taken to complete a function, such as maintaining a record, updating a file, making an inquiry, and preparing a report. The processes further identify the personnel assigned to the system and the flow of data from one person to another and from one step to the next. The process is further broken down into detail procedures. These procedures may be setting up the chart of accounts for general ledger, entering an order in distribution systems, or paying an employee in human resource systems. The Planned Business Process component allows engineers to design improvements and recommend enhancements in the same basic formats used in the original Business Process Definition format.

The specific aim of this component is to model current processes (Ways of Working) and any recommended improvements and present them to the user organization in a desktop environment. The toolset includes scenarios (a series of steps) for major functions that must be performed in a system. The scenarios define opportunities for enhancements. The future user reviews the processes in order from the flow charts. Scenarios define "What" is to be done (see Figure 5.2).

The action (work) statements are outlined with action verbs. Each directs the user to perform the task. Scenarios, as process flows described previously, are linked to these work statements which tell "How" to complete each step in the scenario, and therefore, in the process flow. It identifies each procedure (work statement) by number, and allows users to review the procedure by decomposing down to the procedure. (See Figure 5.3 for an example of a work statement.) This is designed by JAD, in which the engineer or consultant defines the recommended changes, and the user reviews and approves or disapproves of them. Further changes can be made immediately to achieve the best possible design.

Prior to approving a new system or procedure, users should be thoroughly familiar with each function or process for which they will be responsible. Therefore, they review each scenario, referring to the procedures when necessary. In addition, users (and all future users) must be familiar with each procedure or work statement assigned to them when the new system is live. Ways of Working assures that familiarity, and with JAD, allows users to have an active input into the design. Because of its automated features, changes can be reviewed at once in a give-and-take mode.

The major benefit to this component of the implementation engineering tool is the ability to review and adapt the proposed system environment before acceptance and implementation. It can provide management with the comfort that users will understand the system enhancements, their jobs, and their assigned responsibilities before terminating the old system. It is this comfort level that makes this the most valuable aid to implementations ever developed. Business Process Definition greatly enhances the opportunity for successful implementation of user-oriented and user-approved systems and of re-engineered recommendations.

We would recommend quantification of the various processes. Activity-based costing allows analysts to quantify each step or work statement in our lower-level procedures. This was accomplished by entering the following key cost elements at the procedure level: number of transactions, number of persons performing them, and time to complete.

Ways of Working is programmed to access pay rates by job category and compute the time and cost to perform each procedure. The function or procedure is quantified and rolled up to quantify an entire process. Clearly, elimination of steps and procedures could be evaluated based on the economic impact. This is simply an additional capability that is incorporated into a methodology like Ways of Working, where processes are defined by graphical icons that can be accessed and directed to display (or calculate) that which is needed to describe (or quantify).

A related benefit is the ease and cost effectiveness of developing future training courses (reinforcement) based on the new system. The toolset allows design, of course, of scenarios and tests to cover all functionality of a system. Since it utilizes computer-based training software, Ways of Working is not fixed, nor static. Users can impact both the scenarios and the design. Users can add, delete, and modify scenarios and approve new systems recommendations in a JAD mode. This is best accomplished with the tools designed to define our Ways of Working.

Reinforcement or Performance Support

Just to reinforce your understanding of the tool, remember that the basic flow of processes and procedures may be accessed through quizzes and prompts. Reinforcement is possible without separate training programs or in support of separate training courses. If you have defined the process and identified who is to complete the process, if you have documented in procedural format "How" to do that job in the process, then this should be the heart of training which we call reinforcement. It is better known as performance support. It should replace remote classroom training, which does not stick.

Data Identification and Tracking

A comprehensive implementation tool must address both processes and data. The processes are developed in both the Business Process Definition and Planned Business Process Environment components. The Data Identification and Tracking component is concerned with records, data elements, and responsibility. This component addresses the following issues:

- What files or records (hereafter, records) in the system are being re-engineered?
- What data elements are required (and which are merely optional) in work performance?
- Who should be assigned responsibility for the maintenance of records and data elements (hereafter, fields)?

These critical issues and problems must be addressed in re-engineering studies. Normally, customer information services personnel assume this responsibility. They ultimately develop maps and data dictionaries. It is often a costly, error-prone, and lengthy process. Rarely does a software vendor prepare documentation adequately identifying records to be created, fields that are required and those that are optional, and responsibility for records and fields. The Data Identification and Tracking component addresses and resolves these system shortcomings.

This component is integrated with the other implementation components. Files and records are cross referenced to screens and procedures documented in the Business Process components. Using the menu facility of Ways of Working, customers select a specific module (i.e., order entry) and select a specific record (i.e., customer master). The customer may then take full advantage of this component top to bottom (i.e., process to work statement), review data, associate elements with processes, and establish individual responsibility.

This component is programmed in a spreadsheet format under Windows and may be customized. It downloads all relevant records and their associated fields into the PC-based Ways of Working component for identification of the system's data and tracking of the data throughout the system.

Identification selects and automatically prints all relevant records, bypassing temporary work records. The records are then identified in a spreadsheet format, including the following:

- Record name and ID number.
- Record description.
- Number of fields.
- Record length.
- "Key" identification.
- Responsibility (generic department).
- Where used (by module).

The downloaded record also contains information for each field within the record, including the following:

- Field name and ID number.
- Field description.
- Type: Alpha/numeric, Binary, Packed, or Other (user designated).
- Length.
- From and to location in the record.
- Decimal value.
- Occurrence (how many times this field appears, e.g., month would normally be twelve or thirteen).
- Where used or maintained (by screen).
- Where used (by procedure).
- Required or optional or system-generated identification code.
- Comment field (in memo format) to include specific table or code values and general comments.

This information then becomes critical for analysis.

Tracking has two parts. The "where used" information associated with each current record is the first means of tracking the source and use of the record, and the primary field within it. The record contains both its maintenance screen and its primary procedure. In addition, the overall record is "assigned" generically to a department (e.g., the chart of accounts records may be the responsibility of the controller's department).

The second consideration of *Tracking* is referred to as the "new data." The users can input each field of new information and the availability of that data from an existing manual or automated system. The data input should include the following:

- User-source—the source of the field in an existing system (e.g., the inventory file or the manual inventory ledger card).
- User-autocode—whether the user-source is manual or automated.
- User-field ID—to correspond to the new system's field including name, ID numbers, type, length, to and from location, decimal value, and occurrence.

The resulting data are a field comparison of the current and the new.

Data are cost-effective components, designed to reduce errors and save time and resources in the required data-analysis phase of re-engineering studies. Errors are reduced in that records and fields are identified and stored in a retrievable format for analysis and planning. Time and resources are saved, because the lengthy process of identifying records is automated. In addition, the critical data required for conversion specifications are automated and mapped against the availability of current data in a workable format.

Last, setup parameters are an integral part of the data component. BEW, better than others, provides a map of the menus, the configuration of how the system operates. Based on users' settings of options and features, BEW configures the system at a big savings of time and effort for SAP users.

These components work together to reduce the time required by high-level information services technicians to analyze and convert computer records successfully. Therein lies another cost-effective factor of the new implementation engineering tools.

OTHER COMPONENTS

Because of the flexibility of the umbrella software wrapped around the engineering tool, other software components can be accommodated, and at the same time, incorporated into the tool. For example, Microsoft Office incorporates word processing, graphics, a database, and so on to make up an office suite. Ways of Working is no different. The umbrella looms above the various components as a front end to the business processes inherent in the implementation tool. Users can start their day by signing on and accessing their process to define the day's work.

In addition, more software components can be incorporated based on the end result required. For example, we have added a program to our certification software tool (ISO 9000/WOW) that allows users to estimate where they stand in terms of completing the twenty requirements of ISO 9000. We call it the *Gap Analysis*. The Gap Analysis, an interactive spreadsheet application, is accessed from the menu via a predetermined icon.

Another example of component add-ons is a PC-based database of the twenty ISO 9000 requirements. This database, when activated, links the requirements to the existing repository of operating procedures. For example, when ISO 9000 dictates the requirement for a purchasing–receiving procedure to be in place, the engineering model tool allows users to link the requirement to an existing purchasing–receiving procedure. This is the point of multiple views of the same procedure; this is the point of not rewriting procedures for ISO 9000 that already exist in day-to-day operations. This is obtainable only if procedures are documented by a tool like Ways of Working.

A final example of component add-ons is the addition of an activity-based costing component for a client who wanted to evaluate all recommended options in a worldwide re-engineering practice. Because we have documented, in detail, how we work, it is a simple leap to add costing of the individual tasks within a procedure. We simply asked for the number of employees performing the task, the average time, number of occurrences, and average hourly wage rates. To increase the accuracy, we programmed one-time costs and supervisory burden and calculated the cost to perform, rolling up to the next levels of business processes and business modules. It attests to the flexibility of these implementation engineering tools.

CONCLUSION

The recommended approach to improving systems and facilitating re-engineered business processes is to define our Ways of Working, using the new implementation engineering tool. These are the tools that make business processes more visible, assure manageable customizations, facilitate modeling and prototyping, and will be incorporated into a repository of business processes. SAP has launched such a tool, as has Ross Systems with its Strategic Application Modeler, conceived out of the patented methodology we call Ways of Working.

Appendix A shows how Ross Systems developed SAM to define its Ren/ CS manufacturing software. AMR and the Yankee Group have praised Ross's approach. We concur.

11

The Template: Multiple
Views and Best Practices

With these engineering tools, we now have the basis for improvement to adapt the best industry practices and the ability to view processes from multiple perspectives. One single factor in the nature and design of systems has proven to be true time and time again over the years. This observation became the basis for a new approach to the art, not yet science, of systems design and analysis. The observation of reinventing the wheel leads to the conclusion that there is amazing commonality among systems. If that commonality could be captured with flexibility, the difficulties of getting started on a design or revising a process would be reduced. The difficulty in putting pencil to paper, sometimes called the blank-page syndrome, would also be eased. If this commonality could be captured with flexible architecture, the long lead times associated with systems projects could be reduced. In addition, it would be possible to better utilize the specialized talents of the information systems analyst. Moreover, there may be a breakthrough in communications between users and the information services technician. The captured commonality would dramatically affect the systems development life cycle and the use of tools in that process. Finally, there would be a basic format and starting point to truly develop the best industry practices and share improvements among divisions, companies, and industries.

The Ways of Working concept was designed to capture the commonality of information systems. The concept of this approach, simply stated, is to define the critical processes for each major application system. These critical processes define *what* we do; the underlying procedures define *how* we do it. This is a major distinction. Processes define what we do; they normally begin with an event, such as a customer placing an order. The process, then, is defined as the procedures we complete in order to process the order—the business process. For example, when the order arrives, we do the following:

1. Date it.
2. Sort by order type.
3. Look up the customer number and affix to the order.
4. Enter the order into the computer.
5. Print the order.
6. Generate a picking ticket (or manufacturing make order), and so on.

The procedures, then, define *how* we do these things: for example, date it; look up the customer number; enter the order; and generate the picking ticket. It is simple and it is easily explained to users and technicians alike. The process is diagrammed (usually) horizontally and includes unique icons for the major events in the process, including:

- Events.
- Procedures (manual).
- Decisions.
- Procedures (automated).
- Support Processes (e.g., spreadsheets, database procedures).

In the new implementation engineering tools, this is actually the requirement to make business process more visible by modeling the process graphically.

The support, and underlying depth, is to take each procedure and define it as a work statement right down to "press the enter key." The work statement includes the principal inputs, computer screens, and the navigation through multiple screens (or imbedded screens, so to speak). It is the detail of how we work. In the Ways of Working schema, work statements are presented graphically with the logic flow charted and supported by narrative descriptions of the logic, all on one screen. Illustrations will follow.

PROCESSES

The processes that we are picturing graphically are business functions. They are normally clustered by module or organization as follows:

1. *Banking*
   - Demand Deposit Accounting
   - Loan Operations
   - General Accounting

2. *Manufacturing (ERP)*
   - Planning (forecasting, materials requirements planning, master production scheduling, etc.)
   - Execution (purchasing, inventory control, shop floor control, bills of materials, etc.)
   - Measurement (cost accounting, human resources, payroll and labor reporting, fixed assets, etc.)
3. *Accounting or Financial*
   - Accounts payable and receivable
   - General Ledger
4. *Distribution*
   - Order processing
   - Distribution requirements planning
   - Warehousing

Ignoring the cries of "we are different," the concept is to develop the essential functionality of these major applications systems. The development, when completed, will use graphics technology. For years, software engineers have discussed reusable codes as a panacea for long systems projects. Fourth-generation languages use the concept of reusable codes to capture update routines, mathematical routines, and any other common functionality which can be precoded and "reused." Reusable design is now a reality. There was no reason we could not have captured reusable design other than no one thought it possible. The author developed a precursor of reusable design in conjunction with the study of the use of packages in 1990. Now, the concept of reusable design has been developed, tested, and proven with graphics tools at SSA International, Computer Associates, and Ross Systems. The design relies on three concepts in the design of systems: (1) functional partitioning, (2) process flows, and (3) data.

Functional Partitioning

A key element in systems design, and subsequently present in the Ways of Working, is the concept of *functional partitioning*. Systems should not be viewed as monolithic wholes, but are partitioned into those functional disciplines that are its components which satisfy the user's and the *entity's* requirements. We find in today's sophistication, that systems are constantly organized into primary functional processes, which are handled separately and distinctly in this concept. One common way to classify business process is as follows:

1. *Policy*. This is the area of policy decisions that must be made by management, usually one time; in other words, these are not everyday ongoing actions. Examples in order-entry would be credit policy for customers, order policies for

inventory, and so on. Security issues are considered here, as are the authorizations to access secure data. One-time systems issues, such as hardware and communications considerations, are also included in the procedure processing portion of systems.

2. *Activities*. These are the processes (e.g., business processes), which are essential to the business. They may be manual processes, such as receiving an order or issuing a requisition. They may be on-line computerized processes, such as entering a customer order into the order-entry system, inquiring about order status using a terminal, and updating a record indicating the receipt of new stock at the shipping dock.

3. *Period-End*. This is the daily, weekly, monthly, quarterly, and annual reporting and processing. It may be manual processes, such as mailing employee paychecks and filing W-2 forms. It may be computer-related, such as scheduling month-end general ledger trial balances for a batch run.

Figure 11.1 illustrates the three areas of systems for a typical generic customer order system. It is interesting to compare any number of packaged applications software packages against this model; the commonality will become apparent immediately. Those functions pictured in the activity processing section will be similar in each packaged system. They may have different names in Computer Associate's CA-PRMS, as opposed to another order-entry software system, but the functionality will be the same or very similar.

Process or Procedural Flows

A second feature of systems that is common among all is the presence of process flows. Flows are paramount in the Ways of Working. Things are staged and happen in a prescribed manner. The processes, or the way we do things, cross modular and organizational boundaries. They are a combination of manual steps and interfaces with people, resources, and the computer. They are critical elements in the concept of the Ways of Working, and they are literally ignored in most documentation of applications software packages. Software vendor documentation is transaction oriented, not process oriented. The user manual will define input and query screens, what information is needed, what command keys to press, and identification on the next (imbedded) screen. They do not tell you what you are trying to accomplish. Figure 11.2 illustrates what we refer to as this missing link in systems definitions. Typically, we find systems defined in four levels by software vendors as follows:

1. *The Systems Level*. This level identifies each of the modules in a total system. For example, a human resource system usually consists of several modules, such as personnel profile, payroll, applicant tracking, and maybe one other. The system level defines these modular components.

2. *The Functional Level*. This level indicates the major features of the level one modules. In our order-entry example, the functions are invoicing customer maintenance,

FIGURE 11.1
Concept of the Template

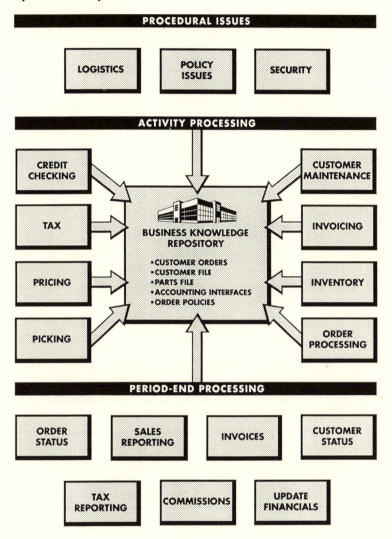

order processing, and so on. No systems description, user documentation, or sales literature is without this functional breakdown of the systems level modules.

3. *The Features Level.* This level of documentation identifies the various features, components, and alternatives available for each function. For example, in the order processing function, there may be several features, such as manufacturing orders, stock orders, make-to-order requisitions, and purchasing orders. These are the finer features within the function and are the basis for the features/func-

FIGURE 11.2
The Missing Link

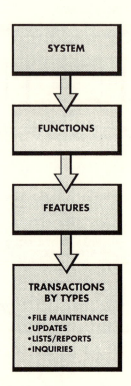

tions madness of applications software packages, package marketers, and package developers—the so called "robust suite of features/functions."

4. *The Transactional Level.* Then we have a list of all transactions that are used to update computer files and records. Invariably, transactions are grouped by categories of file maintenance, updates and action verbs, lists and reports, and file and data inquiries.

We have been challenged on this by some of the largest software developers, and to date, have not been disproved. Almost all user documentation is organized in the manner pictured in Figure 11.2. It was this that allowed us to position the Ways of Working to supplement the systems picture and fill what we believe to be a critical missing link. It was, in part, the shortcoming that necessitated development of the implementation engineering tools.

In the first place, this schema does not reflect the manual processes that are critical to the success of any mission-critical system. This approach simply overlooks the importance of manual interfaces and interactions. This omission is perpetuated in every book we have read on structured analysis as well. Data-flow diagrams, for example, do not include manual interfaces with any level of specificity or clarity. In the second place, critical decisions and decision points are overlooked. What information is available to determine which direction to take? When are decisions required to process an order; for example, is this a regular order or a blanket order, a domestic order or an export? This is a critical omission. In the third place, there are no organizational implications explicit in this schema. Who is responsible for these functions? Who is assigned to use and accomplish the features, such as processing a make-to-order requisition? Who will ultimately use the thousands of transactions that are grouped into file maintenance, updates, reports, and inquiries? Fourth, where is the flow of data and processes? A vice president of a major software vendor on the West Coast asked this when he saw the SAM product at Ross. The thing that has been missing for all these years is the *flow*. In the early years of computers, he recalled, the analysts always prepared flow charts of the processes. Somewhere along the way, that technique was eliminated from the systems description and, until the Ways of Working, was gone.

The process flow is critical in defining how the system will work. We have proven that the process flow is generic in concept. It will, of course, differ somewhat in each specific user or application; the basics remain the same, as we have shown over and over again. The manageability of customization facilitates the alteration of generic to specific.

The president of Cullinet Software (acquired by Computer Associates in 1991) told us that the process flow is the basic fiber of the system. It is so elementary that we (the systems developers) simply overlooked it. Figure 11.3 illustrates how the architecture fits into the standard schema as a new level, filling the missing gap discussed previously. Systems and systems functionality remain. Features and transactions are integral parts of the process. Both are incorporated into the procedural flow and presented by organization and function. Transactions are no longer lists of updates, file maintenance, reports, and inquiries, but are presented as processes in the procedural flow as they are used. It is a logical decomposition:

- SYSTEM (Total–Clusters–Modules)
- SYSTEM FUNCTIONALITY
- THE TEMPLATE
  a. Business Process Flows
     1. Who (Organizations)
     2. How (Detail Procedures)
  b. Transactions

The concept illustrated in Figure 11.3 provides the framework within the methodology for reusable design, which we refer to as the *template*. Decomposing from major modules or enterprise operations to the primary business functions (e.g., process a customer order), we can develop generic templates

FIGURE 11.3
The Template Link

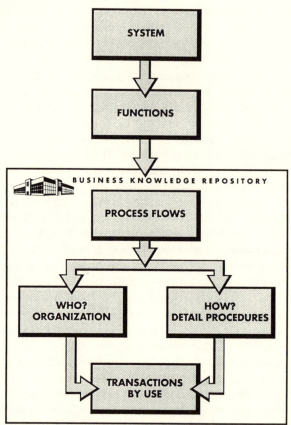

for this functionality. The process begins with an activity or event, as discussed earlier in this chapter. Normally, the first things done are to date the order, sort by type, affix the customer number, and enter it into the system. This is definable.

Based on years of consulting on systems and implementation, a pattern emerges. Using the Ways of Working methodology, we have developed templates for the design and operations of applications in manufacturing, distribution, and finance. Users can benefit from these templates in the same manner that Ross Systems used templates to document their system, Renaissance CS (client–server), and assure the completeness of its design and functionality.

End-users can use these templates to audit operations, re-engineer processes, select applications software packages, or just train. We like the template for all these reasons and because so much good can be gained from reusing accepted practices rather than starting from the blank piece of paper.

The template is possible because there is a structure and a methodology that is applied to original designs, existing designs in the form of packaged application software, and in documentation of day-to-day practices. For example, when we are asked to document an enterprise's Ways of Working, we start with templates, not blank pieces of paper, and ask relevant questions, such as, How do you do this function? The use of templates in the form of reusable design concepts saves dollars and makes sense. It is the second concept in this discussion of systems and design.

DATA

We have always known the importance of data. We call the whole process *data processing*, so there are data and there are people and computers to process it. We think both are equally important. Software engineers have a bias toward data. How often have we heard the following:

- Always start with data, as the rest will follow.
- If you have the data, you can do anything.

The recommended approach relies on a data dictionary of all processes with the data elements of the systems design. It uniquely puts data into context:

- How will the data be used?
- Who will be responsible for the data?
- When will the data be used?
- Where, organizationally and procedurally, will the data be used?

Only in context does it make sense. Years will never erase the memory of that New York banker under a desk full of data-flow diagrams saying, What do I do with this? Years will not erase the memory of an information services director who had cartons of HIPO diagrams, with no possible idea of what they were, how they could be used, or why he had spent millions of dollars developing them—before management literally turned off the computer, processed all accounting manually, and sold out to the competitor.

Data are held in a data dictionary that is correlated to processes, procedures, and transactions. This is the database referred to as the repository in Ways of Working. We can access it via the database, by index, or by glossary. Each has its own icon and access.

THE CONCEPT OF BEST PRACTICES

Drawing on the observation and proof that there is commonality among systems, and understanding the constructs of system's functional partitioning, procedural flow, and data in context, we can produce generic systems designs. Its components are existing techniques, such as business process flow charts, a data dictionary, and data tracking and reinforcement, which we have discussed. Its media is existing graphics and Windows, DOS, and UNIX technology, which we have analyzed and evaluated. Its end product is a methodology that will:

1. Shorten the systems development life cycle.
2. Better utilize the skills of information services management and the technical staff.
3. Include the system user throughout the entire development life cycle.
4. Satisfy users needs through an iterative process of give and take.
5. Increase technical productivity.

By attacking these five lofty goals, the new methodology results in higher quality systems and creates a realistic potential for phased implementation of systems.

CONCLUSION

The concept and methodology resulted from a very pronounced shortcoming in how software vendors supported their users in the implementation of applications software. This shortcoming was mirrored by tradition and practice in large information services departments. The symptom was a lack of communications between users and technicians that resulted in poor implementation efforts, long and unsuccessful re-engineering projects, and excessive and costly misuse of consultants and systems integrators.

Implementation engineering tools are our reaction to this unacceptable condition. Yet, implementation is but one benefit and use of these tools. Equally as beneficial is the opportunity to use these tools for other goals, because the visual presentation of how we work opens up enormous avenues to view work from multiple perspectives. By defining how we work on a daily and period-end basis, we can view our *operations* in a quest to improve and flexibly adapt to new conditions and marketing necessities.

By defining how we work in a meaningful and easily understandable manner, we can map our current practices to the standards and regulations of ISO 9000, QS9000, and the FDA's good manufacturing practices. How often, and at what cost, have we brought in a regulation specialist consultant to "get us certified?" How often have we observed the project when the consultant completely rewrote procedures, as if they were different from the daily ways we work? In a major fragrance manufacturing subsidiary of a Fortune 500 pharmaceutical company, an overbearing project manager insisted that BPCS, the firm's manufacturing system, did not address their ISO 9000 requirements. Overruled, management mapped (not rewrote) BPCS to ISO 9000's twenty standards and found a 70 percent match. Because BPCS is supported by the

Ways of Working methodology (called Business Process Mapping), the process of preparing detail procedures was circumvented because they were already written, in place, and in use. Registration would be a formality as Business Process Mapping became the proof of compliance, not a consultant's heyday of rewritten procedures.

By defining how we work in a way that is visual and manageably customized, we can view operations from an auditor's point of view. A visionary audit partner from a Big-Six firm compiled an auditor's workbench based on Ways of Working. This partner used the graphics capability to define the client's processes and added components to identify the following:

1. Audit control points.
2. Statistical tables for sampling.
3. Organizational responsibilities (in addition to our job description).
4. Audit procedures in graphical form.

Each was important for the client, as junior auditors in subsequent years were not required to redocument existing procedures, merely to audit each. However, the development and documentation of the firm's audit procedures was brilliant. This component, including the processes (what to do) of verifying receivables (for example) and the procedures (how to do it) on what to look for in the verification, greatly reduced training, provided a consistent approach throughout the country, and increased the client's appreciation and comprehension of the audit process.

It is my belief that this view of the audit was so unique that it will encourage other entrepreneurial audits to outsource the audit practice in competition with the Big Six. This view only makes sense in connection with the way clients work. It is a differentiator for those who are not content with the costly practice of auditing procedures that do not change year end and year out. It is an enhancement to a practice that has become a commodity.

These multiple views result, quite simply, from the fact that we have, for once, defined in detail how we work. Once done, we can view work for the following:

- Improvement (re-engineering).
- Training (on-line, real time).
- Implementation (we know how things work).
- Regulatory compliance (nothing is different, just need proof of compliance).
- Auditing (year in and year out).

And whatever else you require. It has always made sense, and now it is feasible.

12

The Design Concept

The new implementation tools are more than just implementation tools. They are primarily interactive design prototyping. It is a more efficient process, however, than that espoused by most systems engineers and referred to as *system prototyping*. System prototyping is the development of the actual system as an alternative to narrative system descriptions. The idea is to build a portion of the system, so users can experiment with the system. According to the experts, the system prototype is an actual application programmed, hopefully, in a fourth-generation language, to show users how the system will work.

With Ways of Working, the user gets a hands-on look at the system through the design prototype and can, through the iterative process, make changes and modifications to screens and reports. It is an excellent view and a working model. The problems of a system prototype cited by the analysts we contacted are fact and perception. System prototyping

- Is a long process that is expensive in terms of analysts and software (fourth-generation languages).
- Merely duplicates the design rather than adds to it.
- Requires different skills than the average designer possesses, that is, programming.

Ways of Working, to the contrary, is a template or design model that differs significantly from a technical prototype. The primary distinction is that the model is not programmed. We shall see that, using graphics technology, the business process is the foundation for code generation, but is a byproduct of the design work. The advantages to this technological approach seem to mirror those of the full-scale system prototype such as

- Reduction in misunderstandings on how the system will function.
- Increased user involvement throughout the systems development process.
- Allowance for quick response on changes and modifications, thus improving the analyst's responsiveness to new ideas and to user contributions.
- Improved design presentation without voluminous narrative descriptions, but workable and addressable solutions.

The model or prototype, which we call Ways of Working, fits well with the desires of leading proponents of new methodologies and improved communication with users. We need to restructure the relationship between information services and users so there will be more communication and mutual contribution. People are trying all kinds of things these days, but no one approach seems to solve all the problems. Initial enthusiasm for the joint application development (JAD) session—a methodology by which information services and end-users get together to flush out requirements for an end-user system—could fade rapidly; for example, if users see it as just another way for information services to retain influence over requirements definitions. You can detect this when users start sending junior representatives to a JAD instead of those representatives with the most to lose—that is, management representatives.

The real problem here is an age-old communication dilemma: Users do not know what to ask for because they do not really know what is possible, and information services people do not know what to offer if they do not really know the business problem to be solved. Formalized life cycle methodologies do not solve this dilemma either. Having the user sign off on a final requirements definition just sets the stage for whom to blame if the system does not do everything the user wants later.

We think interactive prototyping is a promising way to jump this communication chasm. By showing the user screens and functions based on knowledgeable input, both analyst and user may get new ideas on what the system could do beyond the plain vanilla version. Also, the user can give input on what languages his or her people customarily use, so these can be incorporated into screens. Of course, the analyst needs good listening and consulting skills to make this process work. Unfortunately, training for these skills is not a staple on most information services training agendas. The typical requirements session often is a candy store, where users think up all the bells and whistles without worrying about the costs. No wonder they are often shocked when the number comes back. This is often a one-way negotiation, with the only customer option being "take it or leave it." As we have said, Ways of Working is interactive prototyping without the requirement to actually program the system. It depicts process flows, screens, reports, and procedures and is fully supported by data tracking. It provides the visual interface between users and information services in a common language—pictures and flows of actual procedures. It is what we call the framework to communicate, which simply has not existed previously.

A procedural flow is illustrated in Figure 12.1. It describes the processing of a purchase order, creating quotes, and processing returns. The process is presented horizontally and follows the process of activities, forms, and actions. It is generic and is an overview of a typical process called purchase order processing. It will not be exactly the same for each user and will be eventually modified in our iterative give-and-take manner.

Of course, the look is modifiable, and this is but one example. The flow may be horizontal, vertical, or any other way. Some flows list the department and function across the top and the individual procedures under each. This flow distinguishes between departments and functions by using people (stick figure) icons. Either way is appropriate, and in fact, any means of graphically displaying the logical flow of processes is acceptable. But any commercially available flow charting software is not. In order to attain the benefits that we have stressed and comply with the requirements of an implementation engineering methodology, certain criteria must be available. They are as follows:

- *Security.* The user must have the capability to modify these flow processes, but this must be controlled. The implementation tools of which we speak have run-time versions and a development engine. The run-time can be located on a network for review, training, and reinforcement, but the run-time can be changed. The designer, with the development engine, can modify procedures; otherwise, you have chaos.
- *Methodology.* The software supports a specific methodology that structures the business process flows in an organized array of decomposition from a high level down to increasing levels of detail to the lowest level of screens, reports, and data input. Otherwise, two analysts will define the same process differently, a shortcoming, we believe, in the CASE tools. Give two analysts a CASE tool and see what we mean.
- *Decomposition.* The flow chart is a picture of what to do; it must be flexible and able to
    1. Decompose by icon to definitions of how to do each step.
    2. Export to external programs (e.g., spreadsheets) that are inherent in a specific business process.
    3. Incorporate hypertext for word searches and data definitions.
    4. Activate a live session (e.g., through addressing an application program interface [API]).

In addition, the ability to maintain your migration path and return to any level of decomposition is required. These three criteria are critical to the successful development of your Ways of Working and to the strategy we recommend.

The procedural flow puts the function order processing in a context that can be understood by both information services and users. In the many sessions in which we demonstrate the concept, we are *never* accused of confusions or misunderstandings. Flow charting actual operations works, in that it is familiar and the user relates to it. We use stick figures for organizational entities (persons or departments) and the following seven basic symbols or icons:

FIGURE 12.1
The Procedural Flow

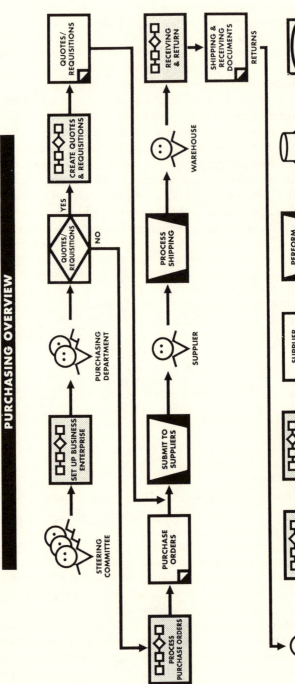

PURCHASING OVERVIEW

1. Process (subprocess)
2. Display (terminal)
3. Database (storage)
4. Person
5. Decision
6. Procedure
7. Document (form, report, etc.)

Clearly, any graphics user interface icons can be substituted for a more contemporary and innovative presentation. With this bag of tricks (icons) we literally define the systems process in an intelligible manner—and in a generic context.

We recently completed a prototype of the inventory and purchasing functions of a fragrance manufacturer and importer. At first, the users complained, Here we go again. It turns out that a headquarters information services analyst had reviewed operations only a month before. The review concluded with documents written in word processing. No one reviewed the work or cared about it. That is why we were there.

There were several shortcomings to the headquarters' approach. First, there was no distinction between processes and procedures. This is a critical failure because processes (what we do) and procedures (how we do it) are quite different. It is a matter of levels of detail with "how" being the lowest level— that is, there is nothing more to say. Second, there were no graphics, and therefore, no incentive to review the accuracy (remember the fun factor). Third, the documentation was not easily accessible.

Our approach was to first define what we do. We used basic icons to define events, decisions, manual procedures, computerized procedures, and sequence of each. The users, not computer literate, were able to review and approve the documented prototype, and then volunteered to define the procedures from their knowledge of how they perform their daily duties. The results were accurate, cost effective, and user controlled. The chief financial officer took this model to (1) recommend improvements, (2) identify duplications and redundancies, (3) question practices, and, most important, (4) identify where to implement computerized procedures using a system they had purchased over a year before, but were not able to implement. The Ways of Working approach makes this possible.

It should be noted that we normally use very few (less than eight) icons. We usually stay with a standard one, such as a diamond to depict a decision point. Yet, if required, the icons can be changed globally; for example, a question mark could be substituted for the diamond to depict a decision point. Icons can be color coded if colors add meaning. Icons can also be programmed (without a programmer) by users to decompose to a lower level of detail. A person icon, for example, can decompose to a job description; a decision can decompose to a decision tree explanation; a procedure icon can decompose to the detail procedure, and so forth.

Each procedural flow is a business function. They overlap modules as order-entry functions interact with accounting, purchasing, and inventory. They are jobs, and jobs interact with other jobs, and this interaction is easily captured in each flow. Each procedural flow may have multiple screens or flows that are easily accomplished with graphics technology. As can be seen in Figure 12.1, the order-processing flow extends to another flow (warehouse), which is identified on the initial chart. These will continue until the entire process is defined completely.

The procedural flow is a consistent methodology which has rules and syntax. Four important rules are as follows:

1. *Direction.* The flow is a singular process that never branches in multiple directions without a process decision.
2. *Organization.* Processes are identified with specific job functions and cannot pass from one job to another without proper notation.
3. *Process flow.* A distinct level in the system hierarchy that cannot appear at different levels; similarly, supporting levels are always consistent within the hierarchy of the patent.
4. *Icons.* Each icon is identifiable and decomposes to a specific view.

UNDERNEATH THE ONION SKIN

The process flow is the primary focus of information in the Ways of Working. Using the capabilities of graphics technology, each icon is described in the design dictionary. A world of power results from this simple mechanical or clerical procedure of defining the icons in the design dictionary. Each icon, now defined, explodes to additional levels of detail (note: specific, not random levels).

Figure 12.2 illustrates this capability to explode to more detail; this is the nesting or decomposition that we described as a feature of graphic tools and technology. The following icons and systems features explode from Figure 12.2:

- Procedure icons explode to detailed procedures.
- Forms explode to the form description.
- Screens explode to screen painter and screen format displays.
- Process flows explode to subprocesses.
- Database icons explode to data element layouts.
- Decisions explode to decision trees.
- Persons explode to job descriptions.

FIGURE 12.2
Ways of Working: Concept of the Template

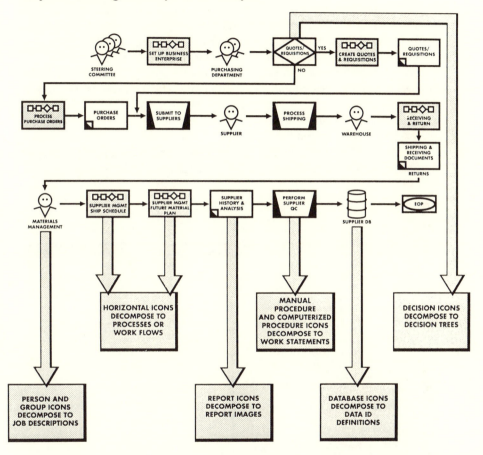

Behind the overview process flow is the complete specification for the system. It is presented in a comprehensive and understandable manner. It defines data within the context of the system by function and by organization. It is simply a better way to present (and design) systems for review, re-engineering, or regulatory compliance.

The *forms* explode and are defined to include common generic formats. For example, a standard government form, such as a W-2, is predrawn or scanned, including number of copies, distribution, and data. More generic forms, such as requisitions and invoices, will be formatted and include the common and essential data required to process the form properly.

Reports explode to indicate format, usage, frequency, and distribution. Generically this is quite possible, although each of these (i.e., usage, frequency, format, and distribution) will change in individual circumstances. It is key to this methodology that the norm is specified in a template, so the end-users must not face the blank sheet of paper, but will modify the business processes to reflect their particular circumstances.

Screens explode to the screen format or screen painter that defines the exact nature and use of the screen. The screens, for example, may consist of a prototype allowing users to enter information to the prototype screen and simulate the screen design and its functionality. The elements on the screen are described in the design dictionary and are thereby linked to data-flows and data stores, assuring consistency of the generic system. The screens may also explode to the system for execution.

Processes explode to specific, generic procedures or work statements in the format illustrated in Figure 12.3. The graphics allows us to picture the

FIGURE 12.3
Detail Procedure

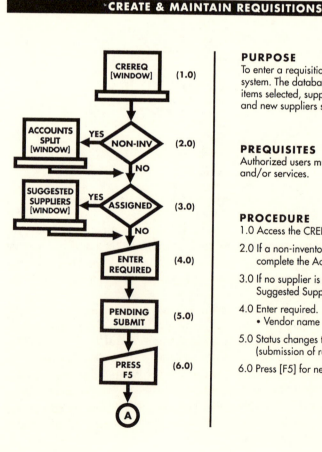

CREATE & MAINTAIN REQUISITIONS

PURPOSE
To enter a requisition manually into the system. The database may be queried and items selected, suppliers recommended and new suppliers suggested.

PREQUISITES
Authorized users must request goods and/or services.

PROCEDURE
1.0 Access the CREREQ window.

2.0 If a non-inventory item, you must also complete the Account Splits window.

3.0 If no supplier is provided, access Suggested Supplier window.

4.0 Enter required.
 • Vendor name and address

5.0 Status changes to [pending submit] (submission of requisition).

6.0 Press [F5] for next window.

specific activities and steps in a process on the left side of the screen and describe the graphics with narrative on the right. This format was developed almost two decades ago and was the one used to sell systems in the 1970s. Now, however, changes do not have to be made with white-out and a photocopying machine. Graphics software allows the analysts to change the activities easily on the left, and just as easily, the narrative on the right. The narrative is a word processor, so blocks of text can be drawn forth in a windowed format and changed as quickly as one can type. It is important in the methodology that the icons used here to describe the activities in the procedure are the same as those in the overall procedure flow from whence we came. This format is always one level below the procedural flow and nowhere else in the methodology. The display icon explodes one level below to the actual screen design or the actual screen. This is the executable screen in the system.

Database icons explode to a data dictionary and the record layout; the database is identified as "customer record," "inventory record," or whatever, and upon exploding on the icon, users can review the generic data elements. For example, the customer record would appear as follows:

Customer Record	*Format*
Name	25 A/N
Account number	5 N
Address, Street	15 A/N
Address, City	15 A
Address, State	2 A
Zip Code	9 N
Credit limit	9 N (99,999.99)

It is important to know that the customer record is recorded once in the data dictionary and can be recalled from any number of procedural flows where it may apply.

Flows among and between processes and other icons (screens, reports, and forms) could, if required, explode to the data-flow diagrams for the systems analysts that we have discussed. By convention, we would select data-flow diagrams and models that most appropriately relate to the methodology. The technique that most closely compliments our belief is one of partitioning and decomposition. It is less crowded in presentation, as it, like the onion, is layered, allowing more detail as one explodes down the processes defined in the Ways of Working. We call this the technical button (or icon).

The structure of all explosions in this implementation engineering tool is consistent. We refer to it as the cell concept. Figure 12.4 illustrates the principle behind this concept. The procedural flow sets on top of a large database of screens, forms, and in Figure 12.4, procedures. The procedural flow illustrated can call on any of the procedure cells as they apply. Similarly, all procedural

FIGURE 12.4
The Cell Concept

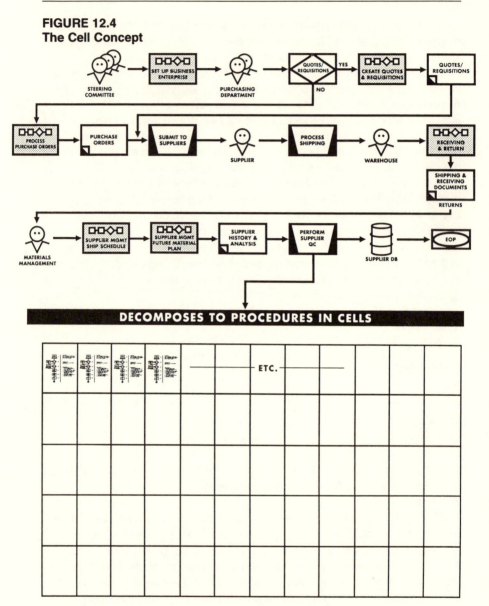

flows within a system (such as order processing) and every function (such as make-to-order) can access the individual screens, reports, databases, and procedures. This is the power available to systems analysts. By defining or modifying the procedural flow, analysts can call any report, screen, procedure, and so on simply by labeling the icon—the design dictionary does the rest.

Therefore, frequently used procedures and screens are stored *one time* here, but are callable by any analyst and any design or any new module or system. This not only assures consistency, but increases productivity by labor years. The cell concept has proven effective over a five-year period of use. It is simple, but powerful, and an enormously effective concept of our Ways of Working.

USE OF THE WAYS OF WORKING

We think of Ways of Working as the beginning of user-based reusable design. Being a generic design of a major system, it has tremendous use as a design aide. It supports all major concepts in the systems development life cycle—planning, design, coding, training, file conversion, and implementation. It is an ongoing design and training concept because it represents operations. It is a design prototype that can be changed as operations change. It is used by the best software developers to document and train on their software. It is a concept whose time has come. Like other ideas that survive as it has over a period of time, it looks good from all angles: It aids the analyst and user alike; it shortens the development life cycle; it may well improve systems quality; and it has ongoing intrinsic value. It makes implementations of packaged software easier, as SAP has shown, and at less cost and time. It facilitates, therefore, implementations of re-engineering recommendations.

In the following chapter, we will review its ancillary uses and benefits and address the systems development life cycle.

13

Using the
Ways of Working Concept

We have concentrated on the new implementation engineering tools, like Ways of Working, as a means to define current business processes. Once complete, the business process becomes the mainstay in implementing new applications software, re-engineering functional operations, obtaining regulatory compliance, training new and temporary employees, and even becoming the base document for costly annual audits. The concept has another major potential; that is, the focal point for new systems design. This was alluded to earlier in the discussion on JAD.

The advantages of using this methodology for design of new systems are obvious. The primary advantage is the ability to prototype (not programmatically) the look and feel of the proposed system quite easily and in a short time frame. Another advantage, as we have observed, is that this methodology facilitates communications between users and technical information services analysts. A less obvious, but equally realistic advantage is that this approach results in simultaneous development of documentation and training as a byproduct of the design. This is revolutionary. It will be welcomed by information services analysts and programmers alike who hate to document their creations.

The use of the engineering tools for design of new systems, however, required rethinking of the old systems development life cycle. The problem with the systems development life cycle is that it is too fragmented. Figure 13.1 illustrates the various steps from conceptual need through programming and testing to an operational system and the inevitable maintenance. Defining business functions as the focal point for each of these steps eliminates the

FIGURE 13.1
Concept of the Template: Old and New Life Cycle

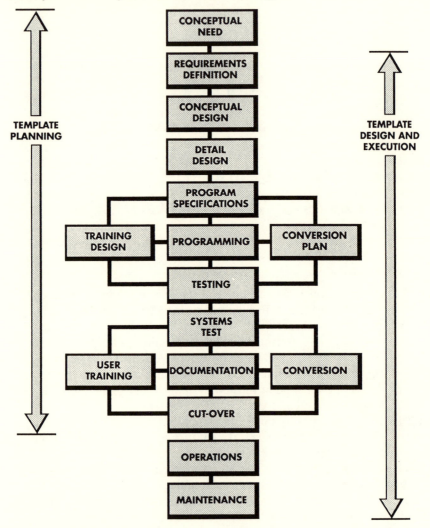

stop–start, freeze-frame approach to systems development. This is basic to Ways of Working.

The key is not only smoothing out and shrinking the systems development life cycle, but the ability to (1) provide an iterative framework, (2) have a new-found consistency with one model or design prototype throughout the entire process, and (3) elevate the information services function to its rightful status and importance within the organization; for information is, in fact, the differentiator in the competitive world where we live. The information here is the graphical business process. Let us discuss how it prevails at each level of the life cycle.

ITERATIVE FRAMEWORK

Ways of Working, being a design prototype of the system from an informational and user perspective, is first the requirements statement, in that it defines operational processes, data, reports, and inquiries. Using this concept at a major international manufacturer, the approach and the result were used to select and evaluate packaged software and to evaluate the potential for developing the system in-house. The format was the same as defined in Chapter 12; vendors responded with notations concerning the availability of each feature and the fit of procedures with the packages. The information services department was able to accurately estimate the time and effort required to develop the system with in-house resources. Management was able to evaluate several software packages and the in-house development as an alternative solution.

Therefore, Ways of Working, being a design prototype, can become the conceptual and detail design. Being a predesigned generic system, it is only necessary for organizations to modify the design to fit their unique requirements. We have spoken of the ease of modifying designs using graphics technology. Here it is clearly seen why we use graphics and why graphics technology was the breakthrough that made the engineering tools capable of visualizing business processes.

The commonality of systems functionality is important in this aspect of the systems development life cycle. It has been shown over and over again that 80 percent of systems functionality is the norm for commonality; this is the rationale that led to software applications packages. This is why we try to determine "fit" and why software developers maintain that 80 percent is a good fit and every customer will probably make 20 percent modifications to satisfy its unique requirements.

Existing templates at Ross Systems or SSA, for example, are 80 to 85 percent on target, we estimate from experience, and therefore, require approximately 15 to 20 percent modification for a completed specific design. But the difference here is that we use computerized graphics technology, and we can easily modify the design. It is a known fact that it is modification of the source code after design that causes the failure of projects, and it is this activity which is costly and escalates all the wrong things such as the following:

- *The analysts' time* in design, program specifications, programming, and testing.
- *The project time* to completion.
- *The cost* of the overall project (remember the toy distributor that is paying more to modify the package).
- *The ultimate maintenance* of the finished product.
- *The risk* of success.

Ways of Working can also be the source of programming specifications. This alternative is left to the user, but the basic generic prototype has sufficient detail to develop the prototype to actually write program specifications. The basic product is tool independent, and although originally developed in Excelerator, it can incorporate many other products.

Training is an integral component of the Ways of Working concept, originating from the procedural flows. Because the procedural flows represent actual operations, and because of the manner in which they are organized—by function and by organization and job descriptions—the procedural flows are the training vehicle as modified to reflect the actual user's environment.

Before going live with the final system, users train on the computer in a "conference room pilot" mode. The scenarios and lessons are the procedural flows; literally, a built-in game plan. The trainees can easily see how they fit into the new procedure as identified by job titles. More important, they can see what activities they will perform in the new system, what documents they will get, what they will do with the data, what transactions are required, and what screens they must know and later work with.

Conference room pilots are training sessions in which each trainee performs his or her assigned tasks, as if it were a live operation. Forms (e.g., customer orders) are received, actions taken (date stamp the order), files are accessed (look up customer number and credit limits), approve and disapprove orders, distribute to other departments and functions, and request nightly batch reports (which are delivered the following day).

It is a most effective way to train or reinforce and to learn a new system or procedure. The training component of the engineering tool provides both the organization (i.e., the individual procedures that must be mastered) and the scripts (the procedural flow) and—the most important aspect—the original documents and prototypes that are being used to assure consistency in approach, continuity in design and training, and cost effectiveness, as a result of not having to develop new training materials and lessons. Because we integrate graphics software that looks like computer-based training software, we develop quizzes and prompts that ask the questions and then allow users to either select the correct answer or be prompted to the correct answer. The architecture keeps test scores and certainly keeps track of who has been trained, when, and how well they did. This, of course, is a major requirement for systems supporting operations requiring regulatory standards and certification.

The same is true of documentation. The process flows, once modified, are the user documentation. It quite literally can (and should) be the user documentation. When the founder of a large software developer saw a graphics-based procedure we once presented to him, he commented that with this methodology—his company could finally get out of the user manual printing business. We have subsequently seen an entire organization train on our graphics procedures, to the exclusion of training and user manuals. Not only is it more complete than a normal manual, it is

- *Better organized* by functions within organization and job description.
- *More comprehensible*, beginning at a high level of understanding and decomposing to finer levels of detail.
- *More accurate*, reflecting—after modification—exactly how the system will function in the user's environment, including correct form names, report names, and unique nomenclature.
- *Measurable* with the student database.

Serious observers believe that Ways of Working is a better means to document systems. We often refer to it as our big "help screen," and we are not often challenged on that point.

Conversion planning and actual conversion processing (i.e., converting one database structure to another) is facilitated. Once again, drawing from the single design prototype, the tool identifies each data element in the system, organized by file and by record layout. Each data element, it will be recalled, is defined in the Data Identification and Tracking components. This allows us to list the data elements and identify, through the where-used facility of spreadsheet technology, where data elements are used by procedural flow, by detail procedures, and by screen or transaction. For conversion planning, we list each data element in a spreadsheet format as follows:

Data Element	Data Format	New System Usage	Current Source
XXXXXX	XXXXXX	XXXXXX	_____
XXXXXX	XXXXXX	XXXXXX	_____
		XXXXXX	_____
		XXXXXX	_____
XXXXXX	XXXXXX	XXXXXX	_____

Ways of Working provides a listing of the data elements and their usage in the new system (i.e., which procedures and transactions). The information services staff, with the user, defines where that particular data element is to be found in the current system whether manual, in another system, or nowhere to be found. Supporting data-flow diagrams could become the basis for the actual programming, if desired.

The end product "deliverable" from this data element analysis is a conversion specification. The data-flow tables indicate the source and usage of data; the user analysis provides the guideline to where the information is available in the current environment. The template remains, once again, the vital cog in the systems development life cycle. Data conversion specifications and planning are completed using the single design prototype we call the Ways of Working.

Planning is facilitated by this comprehensive engineering tool. This is because of the simple reason that it is easier to plan what you know. It is easy to see what processes must be put into place, what procedures must be implemented, what screens and reports are required, what conversion programs must be programmed, and generally, what lies ahead. Using project management software, we are able to set out the detail tasks that are required to implement a full-scale module. Timing and tasks differ, of course, depending on whether in-house development is planned. Nevertheless, basic tasks and a project plan are more easily developed from the information available in the repository of systems, processes, and procedures.

We have concentrated in the past on Microsoft's Project and Super Project from Computer Associates in Islandia, New York. But other project software may be just as appropriate. We do not recommend any one software product, but do recommend use of a computerized project management system. The template, then, is the guideline for developing the individual tasks. The plan component is the software used to plan the project, accept work against tasks, and report to management. Our southern client was unable to develop a plan in four months. Using our procedural flows in an early version of this concept, this manufacturer completed its plan in three weeks and presented it to management. It is possible when you know where you are going and are using this approach as your road map.

Finally, Ways of Working and the other engineering tools are the operational guidelines, as they uniquely reflect the way the system will operate. Unlike any methodology to date, or any implementations strategy or product, the Ways of Working is a live entity, reflecting not how a system will be installed alone, but how it will be used daily, weekly, and monthly. It is now a critical element in the decision to change and improve; it is critical in analyzing weaknesses that may crop up; it is the essential element in the training of new employees. It is the basis for re-engineering.

ONE MODEL CONCEPT

Three very important attributes of Ways of Working should now be evident. They are as follows:

1. *Continuity.* One design prototype using one method has sufficed as the control and design media from inception to operation. Think of it:
   - The design document is the user documentation.
   - The user documentation is the basis for training, using this conference room pilot technique and EPSS/Reinforcement.
   - The inherent design dictionary and auxiliary data-flow diagrams are the source of conversion planning and specifications.
   - Operations are monitored by the prototype originated at the inception.
2. *Iterative approach.* One model or prototype throughout the process assures that users can be involved at every critical stage with iterative conversations, using a media that both information services and the end-user understands and contributes. Organizational barriers dissolve as the whole process can be viewed seamlessly.

3. *Efficient.* The one-model approach assures that there is no recreation of the wheel, as each stage builds on the previous one. It is our belief that new systems can be programmed and operative within ninety days routinely. This is because the Ways of Working is a reusable design with the whole implementation in mind.

RESULT—ELEVATES INFORMATION SERVICES

We have found that proper use of this prototype of reusable design with all of its supporting components can raise systems and the information services function to the position of importance it requires. For the first time, the information services director can have a comprehensive look at information processing in the organization—seamlessly over and through organizational divisions and barriers.

Three professors from Auburn University recognized this best. They observed that most of the knowledge concerning how the business functions and how information serves the business resides in the minds of a relatively small group of people in the enterprise. In addition, the design of business systems (if known at all) resides in the minds of a few key information services personnel. Very little information concerning how business systems function is directly related to the software supporting business operations. Information regarding how business systems function describes the following:

1. The business enterprise and its departments.
2. The environmental conditions facing the business.
3. Department operations.
4. Why the operations are important.
5. Why operations are performed in a certain manner.
6. Why certain information supports operations.
7. How the information is used.
8. Why certain conditions influence operations.
9. What information concerning these conditions is needed and why.
10. Responsibilities for operations.
11. Job functions of personnel.
12. How and why information serves these job functions.

Graphics systems, like Ways of Working, provide a means of permanently storing, reviewing, and updating this important information. This information is stored within solution-oriented models. The information in these models symbolizes the knowledge of key business personnel in an effort to better secure and more extensively use this accumulated knowledge. Once stored, this information may be shared with other key personnel in the business. Thus, a graphics-supported environment provides additional methods for securing knowledge and making it more readily available within the firm.

The Ways of Working addresses all twelve issues about information, and it describes how business systems function.

We agree with the Auburn professors and note that the new wealth of information and data compiled by us and using existing software will enhance information services' position within the management structure. This is as it should be. Now information services can contribute even more to the competitive position of the enterprise, because we all know that information can be the differentiator in the competitive environment where we live. The Ways of Working is information organized to reflect the organization.

CONCLUSION

We see this, and other implementation engineering tools, as a powerful tool in the information services arsenal, which illustrates the potential we see for use of the product. There are several primary areas where the approach is being used today. They are as follows:

- *Defining Requirements and Designing a System.* The key is the existence of reusable design that can be compared to user requirements and as the design document. It is being used now by a software vendor to develop an order-entry system. It enhances the concept that in-house design is a viable alternative to packaged software.

- *Re-engineering Operations.* In Europe we will use the order-entry template to compare an existing system to the generic "ideal." The concept is to have a blueprint for improved efficiency. Similarly, the Ways of Working is applicable as an audit tool; we call it the auditor's tool kit. It allows third party, outside auditors to identify control points (or lack of them) in its client base companies.

- *Integration Services.* Ways of Working is the recommended methodology for consulting integrating systems. The initial step in this process is to map existing systems and interfaces. No tool better fits this requirement than the Ways of Working. Its ability to define processes and data, decompose to more detail, and project to additional procedural flows—regardless of module integrity—uniquely says that this is the approach to integration consulting, just as we pointed out earlier in regard to Lockheed's tower of Babel argument.

- *Business Documentation Software.* Three major software vendors use it to document their business systems. The systems are documented generically, and users can easily re-engineer their system or their processes and develop their own user documentation. EPSS training, implementation planning, and data identification and tracking are included. Appendix A is a sample of this use by Ross Systems. Ross incorporates data tables as well in its Ways of Working.

- *Stand-Alone Documentation.* Ways of Working is used to define stand-alone systems and processes. HelpMate 9000 is an example of a Ways of Working product that defines many processes including the quality certification process necessary for enterprises that want to market in Europe or sell to companies that market in Europe.

These examples are only the tip of the iceberg. One recent example is further study of expert systems to show interfaces with procedural flows. These examples show we are designing means by which management can examine processes and then identify the exact systems and functions that must be optimized to realize business objectives. It is possible because application software and information is captured in methodology and can unlock the answers. How should management focus on using this concept? One target is the chief financial officer who can appreciate the impact on cost and business efficiency.

14

The Visionary CFO— Managing Change

The visionary chief financial officer (CFO) looks at the enterprise and not the pieces. As one top IBM executive has said, Management does not wake up saying we need a new operating system, but rather, how can I make my enterprise more successful. Often, this was difficult because it was not a certainty that the CFO truly understood how things worked in his or her company. Obvious and understandable reasons could include the technical complexity of products and processes, staff turnover, recent downsizing, departmental walls, and information barriers, to name just a few. Recent acquisitions of a division or an entire new company also posed a legitimate reason why the CFO did not have a complete grasp on operations.

This situation has been costly in terms of total, as well as redundant efforts, long and unsuccessful implementation projects, disruptive regulatory compliance mandates, board of director dictates on merging operations, re-engineering, downsizing, and stagnant productivity measurements. There is a commonality to all of these efforts and an opportunity for the CFOs to impact each in order to "make the enterprises more successful." The common element in these is the ability to manage change. New implementation engineering, such as Ways of Working, provides the tools and methodology to manage change in a common way.

To manage change with the Ways of Working, for example, requires a type of vision that is not usually available in the day-to-day trenches of the information services analysts. It requires experience facing the responsibility for implementing new solutions, complying with new regulations, coping with top management dictates, and answering to dismal productivity statistics. To manage change requires a commitment to define the way we work in a meaningful and useful manner that can be visualized, modified easily, and communicated to a diverse set of users, management, and information services technicians. But to do so can result in the benefits that are attainable using methodologies and tools that are now available.

Managing change starts with understanding what is to be changed. A large manufacturer that recently encountered problems during the testing stages of an application developed by a team of vendors, found that the vendors and in-house groups had each been interpreting the current processes differently. The user group in charge of the project noted they were discussing each of the tasks in the language of the specialists, the in-house information services group, and vendor. There was no communication.

But these users were creative and called a management meeting, during which the user group showed a chart that pictured a driver following a path that led from one sign in the international traffic sign language to another. One showed a picture for a restaurant and another showed a picture for an airport. Management stated that they wanted a set of pictures like that which described the functions of the proposed new application, and they wanted to be able to relate each of the tasks that produced, tested, and installed applications to those pictures. The approach, developed to meet the needs of management and the user group, was a combination of process flow diagrams that could be shown on PC screens and procedures that instructed users how to relate to those screens to project tasks and its usefulness to management. This is an illustration of the Ways of Working.

This approach toward developing, designing, and defining processes, as well as documenting and training for application systems use enabled management and users to more easily establish the base for the new information systems application. The new application could then be more easily quantified, monitored, and measured after implementation. This could be done because the graphics model was an implementation engineering methodology called Ways of Working, that can describe existing functions or the design of an application which would meet new functional requirements. The graphics model can be matched to statements of requirements and objectives. It helped to assure an effective and successful implementation project. For the visionary CFO, it revealed new possibilities for resolving problems he or she faced in making the enterprise more successful. The CFO realized that the knowledge gained in this one area could be extrapolated to the enterprise and would be absolutely essential in helping to manage change. Opportunities for using the methodology included regulatory compliance, downsizing mandates, and productivity problems.

REGULATION COMPLIANCE

First, the CFO addressed regulatory compliance; six graphical representations were developed to show the process of ISO 9000 registration. ISO 9000, of course, is the international standard for developing a quality program. Once a marketing nicety, ISO 9000 is now a marketing necessity if you want to do business in Europe or if you sell to an enterprise that does business in Europe.

ISO 9000 is a process and processes are easily described graphically and very difficult to describe in a narrative. In the graphical process flow of Ways of Working, an overview illustrates the process in which the steering committee undertakes "initial planning." This generates two deliverables: policy statement and organization chart.

A second phase, "audits and documents" current procedures, with a quality manual as the deliverable. This overview decomposes (explodes downward) into more detail. For example, the "initial planning" icon decomposes to a second illustration, which defines in more detail the process of initial planning. Using this, the steering committee can perform the following tasks or procedures:

- Define policy.
- Review ISO 9000.
- Perform a preliminary survey.
- Conduct ISO 9000 assessment.
- Evaluate the results.

The possibility of proceeding further in exploring processes is illustrated, for example, with a "Ready" indication that questions whether the enterprise is ready to proceed to the next step of "Establishing Documentation Standards." In the methodology called Ways of Working, each of the icons further explodes to procedures on how to accomplish the task. The processes, therefore, describe step-by-step *what to do* (in this case, initial planning), and the next level of detail explains *how to do it*. The process flow tells users to Define a Quality Policy, and the next level describes how to write this policy.

It is noteworthy that each icon will explode to a lower-level definition. For example, in the Overview, the deliverables, which are a policy statement and an organization chart, explode to the real policy statement and an organization chart that defines the responsibilities of the organization in the ISO 9000 certification process. The last icon in Initial Planning allows you to proceed to the next process, which is Internal Audit and Documentation. This process is shown in the third graphics representation. By now, management can understand that the last icon on that representation allows them to proceed to the next process, Assessment, the fourth graphic representation. The fourth proceeds to the fifth, Final Assessment and Registration, which in turn proceeds to the final step in the process, which is Continued Improvement.

This is an example of the graphics capabilities of these implementation engineering tools that appealed to the CFO. Processes are pictured and supported by narrative. At the business process level, they define processes or what to do, while they lead through decomposition to the next level, which defines how to do it. Forms, screens, and reports can be identified at either level and shown to users and information services personnel at will or at the click of a mouse.

The icons can be directed without programming to explode to scanned reports, captured screens, and detailed procedures (work statements). They can also be directed (without weeks of training) to pick up PC-based software, such as spreadsheets and word processing. How would you use this architecture? Insert the spreadsheet program, for example, as it is used in the day-to-day operation. Your day-to-day operation may be to perform certain tasks, such as processing customer orders, but at some point, use a special spreadsheet to review customer orders. You or other users can trace this customer order process, explode on the icon, and access the actual spreadsheet program. This not only puts the spreadsheet program in perspective of when it is to be used and for what purpose, but it also allows access to the actual program. Ways of Working can become the front end for use of spreadsheets and database applications.

With the Ways of Working concept, the CFO and the regulators can walk through what amounts to a visual picture of the system that illustrates how each function and activity is carried out. These functions and activities demonstrate how each regulatory requirement is met. It is self-explanatory to FDA and ISO registrars. Management can confirm that standards will be met by the functions that are implemented, because the registrar can review how the flow of data and activity in the graphic documentation of how these functions meet requirements and accomplish the regulatory objectives. The requirements, and the objectives that the requirements support, can be referenced to the functions and modules in the graphics documentation to aid monitoring of development and confirmation that results have been achieved. This also shows how future improvements are possible, monitorable, and reachable.

To make the regulatory compliance easier and to reduce the overall cost of the registrar's audit, the CFO was able to list all ISO 9000 standards and link them to the procedures dynamically. Therefore, when the registrar demanded proof of a policy statement, a link had been made to the appropriate procedure and the actual policy document. Similarly, when requiring proof of purchasing procedures, the auditor could access the Enterprise Resource Planning (ERP) system and the actual purchasing procedure. In this case, the ERP system was BPCS from SSA-MidAtlantic (Rochelle Park, New Jersey). BPCS is fully supported by Ways of Working (under the trademark of Business Process Mapping [BPM]).

The point here should be clear. This CFO did not write new procedures for ISO 9000 certification. Because those procedures were already written in detail in BPM, the CFO simply had to link the ISO 9000 standard to the BPM (BPCS) procedure to prove compliance. The concept is applicable to all regulatory compliance. BPM, for example, supports ISO 9000, QS9000, FDA, and Malcolm Baldridge National Quality Awards with its hyperlinking capabilities (i.e., an integral feature of advanced implementation engineering tools). The CFO benefited from the BPM (Ways of Working) approach of the following:

1. Linkage to quality requirements.

2. Linkage to verification documents (e.g., policy statement).

3. Identification of quality responsibility (organization component).

4. Process definitions (glossary of terms component).

5. Training scores and proof of attainment (training component).

THE YEAR 2000 PROBLEM

The year 2000 problem is well known. Millions of lines of code are being analyzed by COBOL programmers to identify where dates will cause problems. It has been identified as a multibillion-dollar problem. Management is objecting to budget allocations by information systems to fix the problem that can be over 50 percent of total information services budget. Ways of Working can be a valuable tool in defining the problem areas, justifying the cost, and preventing disasters.

Defining the Problem

Information systems is editing its COBOL code, finding retired COBOL programmers, and searching the code for dates. Even when dates are found, the programs may be obsolete and, worse, not even used. It is a nonfocused and expensive process. It would be better to define the Ways of Working with applications and identify where dates are entered, used, and output *from the user's perspective*. This would focus the code search dramatically and enable management to decide where date problems need to be recoded and where the process is old and needs changes.

Justifying the Cost

A stand-alone project for the year 2000 is hard to justify. Management contends that this problem should never have arisen. Why did MIS not take care of it before? Why is it so expensive? To resolve the year 2000 problem using the Ways of Working model, on the other hand, makes sense. There is a benefit to the organization from studying and solving the year 2000 problem, just like ISO 9000 can be a byproduct—*not* the sole objective.

Preventing Disaster

Since you can use Ways of Working as an umbrella or graphic user interface front-end, you can prevent use of specific screens and procedures until the affect of dates is analyzed. If a problem arises, management can control access to the problem process and procedure, thus preventing disaster.

IMPLEMENTATION OF NEW SYSTEMS

Failures and cost overruns are common. A review of the SAP system which emphasized its complexity has been discussed. For the CFO, implementations require managing change. The visionary CFO will use, just as SAP recommends, an implementation engineering model to assist in managing the project.

Management and users together can refer to a graphics template of functions to immediately learn the system requirements and understand the objectives that must be achieved when a set of modules or a subsystem is implemented. They can do this by referring to a Ways of Working model and asking if tests confirm that certain steps in the model have been achieved. Management and users can also understand what requirements and objectives are delayed or at risk if certain functions are delayed or cannot be fully achieved with the computing hardware, software packages, network capabilities, or other system components being used. Time frames can be quantified using the activity-based costing component at the same time and method as costs are quantified. The CFO can manage the project better using this model.

A set of narrative requirements and a system design prepared by an information services staff can be utilized by users or management as support to the graphics documentation. But management cannot easily visualize what requirements are and how automated and manual functions will fit together to satisfy requirements and meet business objectives without illustrating process flows graphically. Even if the users and CFO are walked through the requirements and design by the information services staff or a consultant, and they annotate the documents to indicate how objectives will be met, they are not left with an approach that they can use by themselves to monitor or investigate when and if objectives are achieved. The implementation engineering model fills this gap, and includes the planning component.

As discussed, the Ways of Working model also answers the major questions on project status, such as whether the requirements and functional design that were established at the beginning of a project will achieve objectives and whether the functions that are implemented satisfy requirements and objectives. Ways of Working also has the capabilities of monitoring progress and auditing activities. There are a number of questions that can be asked on a regular basis about the schedule of tasks to be done. Regular reports from a manual or automated project management, control, and reporting system are used to satisfy this need. The task numbers and names that are fed into the project management system are cross referenced to the functional tasks and activities in the graphics documentation, as shown in the following list. The project management reports can be related to specific functions and requirements that are being satisfied, and which are indicated in that document.

Task 101	Set up Customer Master
Task 102	Set up Terms and Term Codes

Task 103   Set up Ship-To Files

Although manual project reporting could be used to develop the task list shown, the variety of automated project management systems now available makes it worthwhile to consider using one of these products. There are sophisticated project management systems available for use on PCs that can be run on the same system that is handling the graphics model for the project. Popular project management products such as On-Target, Microsoft Project, SuperProject from Computer Associates, or Timeline could be used. For larger projects, a product such as Project Scheduler 4 could be used. The list used an example that could have been based on one of these products.

The combination of the graphics documentation provided by the Ways of Working approach, annotated to show which functions meet specific requirements, and the use of a project management system referenced to the documentation provides management with perspective, overview capability, and monitoring.

The graphics documentation of Ways of Working is used by management to relate the business objectives behind systems projects to other business plans in a company. Systems projects might be implementing new order-entry, reporting sales, and budgeting systems to support a business plan that is changing marketing and sales from a set of five national groups that each support a different type of product to regional groups that will handle all products on a regional basis. In addition to the new or modified computing applications that will be needed to support these plans, reorganization of personnel, changes of offices and facilities, changes in equipment supply and support, planning for purchasing, and a number of other activities must be carried out.

In addition to using project management tools to help with the implementation of these plans, the graphics documentation of Ways of Working can be used to portray what activities have to be done and in what stages to achieve objectives, as illustrated in the following list:

Plans to Achieve	*Visual Ways of Working*
Cost Savings	Cost Matrix
Cycle Time Reduction	Before/After Flows of the Cycle
Improve Training	Performance Support Results
Activities to Achieve	
OE Project Completion	Plan/Milestones
AR Goals Set	Plan/Goals
Goals to Achieve	
Cut A/R Balances	Dunning Procedures
	Aging Reports (Graphics)

The Ways of Working approach improves the ability of the CFO to manage by objectives that can be applied to the implementation of manual or automated systems or any set of activities that achieve business objectives. In each case, the starting point must be dictated by management, and logically the CFO should define current practices and organize them into a repository of processes and procedures.

This is desirable since Ways of Working is an approach to problem solving that facilitates planning the steps being taken in support of corporate objectives, as well as for solving information systems application problems. It focuses on the need to start an exercise in problem solving with an easy-to-understand overall view of the problem, together with views of the sections or parts that make up the problem that can be decomposed from processes to procedures. This has been difficult because processes cross organizational lines, and one unit may not know what another is doing.

These cross-organizational views can now be linked together in a package or framework that business managers can use rapidly to investigate a problem, such as the selection and modification of a vendor software package for an order-entry system to serve a new product offering. The linked view could be the modification of an existing computer application to support changes in part ordering and supply for a product assembly operation that will speed up the ability to respond to customers. Management can view these two problems as before and after processes.

Ways of Working provides a framework for communication that is like a package of pictures or slides for browsing through or jumping around in a business problem and devising a solution to it. It is possible to make notes on these pictures to indicate where they should be changed to describe the business problem better or have the processing accomplish new requirements. A 1993 *Harvard Business Review* article called "Attach Yourself to an Order," recommended following an order from receipt to shipment. It pointed out the problem of crossing organizational lines; no one knows the total process. This was a call for Ways of Working and a clear recognition that department management does not now know the entire process, because they had no tools or methodologies to grasp it before this development.

It is easier for business people to think about reviewing a set of pictures that illustrates how something is now done in order to decide what must be changed to implement new business systems. Ways of Working provides such a visual solution. We can display the process seamlessly, so management can understand, question, and improve this critical order management process or attach itself to the order and take charge of the project.

COPING WITH THE BOARD

Now we will deal with the problems facing CFOs when management or the board of directors dictates change. This may be in the form of downsizing to meet corporate financial goals or re-engineering studies because one outside director has just learned a new approach to profit improvement. The first step, of course, is to define the objectives clearly, although we know they are cost-related. Then the CFO should go to the repository of processes and procedures to see what is involved. Please note: If such a repository does not yet exist, it is the first step as visualized in the implementation engineering approach of Ways of Working.

A functional model, such as AMR's supply chain operations model, of how things should be done is a good start. Efforts to write a thesis and documentation of requirements or the functions to achieve improvements, particularly when prepared by systems analysts, can be tedious for management to follow. It is a challenge to skip back and forth in a written document to review the procedures that describe how something is done. There is much less willingness or time available for senior managers to review additional written documents today. Graphics models are essential for re-engineering and other systems projects. One CFO is now documenting the purchasing process for a large flavors company with such a model, and is confident of the results that will be obtained.

At this flavors company, a committee was set up to improve operations, both manual and computerized. The ERP system was developed and marketed by JBA Software Products Limited. The CFO started with the receiving function, which crossed various departments, including purchasing, warehousing, and quality assurance. The first task was to define what the company does and to help users narrate the process accurately. Using a graphics model with only a few simple icons to identify manual procedures (e.g., forward a document), JBA computerized procedures (e.g., generated the purchase order), decisions (e.g., return to vendor or not), and personnel tasks (e.g., receiving clerk). The model successfully defined the steps, events, and decisions required to process a receipt.

The CFO simply set the stage interestingly and defined the approach. The flavors company's user personnel took over and defined the business process since they understood it best. That is what has been advocated throughout this book.

The result was that the committee could clearly see duplication of effort, some unnecessary steps, a poor use of planning because of a breakdown in purchasing, and a better way to use the JBA system. Furthermore, it was easy for the committee to communicate the problems and the solutions to management, who could see the problems and the recommended improvements through the use of the model. Of course, because we had captured the tasks and supported them with procedures and detail work stations, it was an easy step to cost each procedure using the activity-based costing component of Ways of Working software to convince management on the desirability and cost benefits of implementing the recommendations. The use of consultants was minimal in relation to the savings, because the consultant only consulted, the users defined the current process, and each of them and the committee formulated the recommendations.

The ability for management to visualize steps, trace business functions from one department to another, and annotate or make changes to the functions favors the use of PCs. It also requires that the graphics techniques and the words used with them to compose the pictures be chosen, so the results can be followed by any businessperson from CFO to clerk. The development of this capability required tools and methodologies and the knowledge of how to present information. Logical flows are easier to develop for a functional department than the use or preparation of standard written documentation. This is the heart of the Ways of Working concept and the way CFOs can manage change effectively.

The use of icons and graphics documentation to describe functions to be automated and the functional design for new applications, together with interfaces to systems development and software engineering tools to build and test the applications, is the basis for the new methodology. It is easier to define processes graphically because there is a logic supported by visualization that is difficult to impact with words. The graphics documentation is more useful, too, since it can then be used for design, re-engineering training, and as a prototype for the application that will allow users to test how it will function and suggest modifications if needed.

As described, the graphics documentation by itself can be used for planning corporate business programs or conversions to new information services technology or other purposes, simply because it is the framework for communications between information services and line management, and because it can define current practices as we know them.

The CFO, by using this approach, can also have a major impact on corporate training, which is critical in responding to plans for downsizing or acquisitions. It never made sense to have one person design a system, another document it, and a third train personnel on using it. Management has paid for this approach. Ways of Working uniquely addresses this anomaly. The design document is the documentation and the basis for training—all in one. If the business processes are presented in the format described herein, with process flows exploding down to procedures with screens and reports, it can solve the problem of communicating the design to users. Thereafter, it is in sufficient detail to become the user documentation. It describes work statements thoroughly. This is true whether you are designing a system or implementing a software application system. In the latter, of course, the vendor must be using the implementation engineering model described. This model is the vehicle for training. In a climate of downsizing, management must be concerned with training. Fewer must do more, and therefore, they must be trained.

Training in the Ways of Working model is patterned after the concept of performance support systems, as discussed previously. The Ways of Working model provides the detail needed to define a job in detail and in context to the overall business process; that is, placing an order or preparing the trial balance for the general ledger. Management must position this documentation as the basis for training. Remote training and independently developed training courses will not suffice.

Business process training can be supported with quizzes, tests, and prompts. This allows users to be tested in a rather fun-oriented environment that is close to the real world. Questions, of course, can be true or false, key word, key phrase, or multiple choice. Responses to user answers can be narrative, audio, video, or animation in the implementation engineering model since it has multimedia capabilities. Processes like ISO 9000 require that we keep track of who has been tested and with what results. This is clearly within the scope and definition of Ways of Working—it is within management's mandate to provide a skilled and trained employee.

Prompts are valuable adjuncts to the training component. You can prompt a user through a process by asking questions and prompting (or providing) the answer. In both prompts and quizzes, users may access their original graphics of processes, procedures, screens, organizations, and job descriptions. Therefore, the quizzes and prompts merely support the understanding of the processes and work statements—all of which are accessible and do not require redrafting for training. They are windows and are addressable if users need to reference them. We believe prompts can be developed for temporary employees to quickly and cost-effectively train them when they are required. This again is an enormous opportunity for the CFO to have a major impact on company productivity and the bottom line.

The use of the implementation engineering model not only assures that business processes are communicated more easily and are more likely to be achieved, it can help information systems projects to be accomplished with more control and productivity. The documentation of requirements can be done more rapidly in a graphics rather than a written form. Documentation of a functional design for a project can also be done more rapidly with the graphics model. The graphics model of the application can be used to assist in training and testing, since it describes the functions that the new system must achieve. The graphics model can also be used as a prototype to test out application concepts before implementation takes place. The graphics documentation tool in the implementation engineering model aids with automated analysis and design and application generation.

PRODUCTIVITY

Productivity is the amount, in dollars, that a worker produces in a given hour. Productivity in this country has been stagnant, growing at about 1 percent annually. Computers, being only 2 percent of net investments by businesses, have not contributed as much as possible.

Productivity can be impacted by using computers to develop graphics models of processes and the functional design of the application through the use of templates that provide a starting picture for the type of application involved.

Users can start with one of these graphics diagrams and customize the picture of the application involved (such as an order-entry system for a distributor), until it matches the unique situation needs of the company. The work of AMR in its Supply Chain Operations reference model could be the beginning of AMR development of templates for banking, distribution, manufacturing, and accounting applications. Such templates may be available soon. Using graphics technology to provide the capabilities and benefits described could provide AMR and others with significant cost savings and opportunities.

The main benefits of the Ways of Working concept have been proven in its actual use:

1. The introduction of an easier means for business people to specify and review what computing applications should do.
2. Productivity improvements in developing the application system to meet the functional needs of users.

The graphics model also provides the opportunity for users and information systems personnel to use graphical means of describing requirements and developing applications that current trends indicate will become more utilized in the future.

Ways of Working is an approach that supports two important needs that will have an impact on applications. One is the need for greater use of software engineering tools to analyze problems, design solutions, and generate applications. The other is that the current techniques of software engineering, including reverse engineering, will permit graphics tools to communicate with users in the analysis and design of applications.

Although the previous tools were not always user-friendly or business-oriented enough to meet current needs, Ways of Working provides the base system design to reduce the blank paper syndrome and further the design effort as the framework for communication. It is presently used with a number of software engineering methodologies and tools, including those that generate codes.

The final need which the template supports is the increasing use of business process re-engineering in commercial applications. Many projects now involve the use of components from more than one system, and the overall view becomes increasingly important. Corporations are chiefly motivated to do this type of analysis because they feel their needs cannot be met solely from the experience of one department or function. This allows additional resources to be applied to problems, another factor that has proved to be important.

When more than one function is used to implement applications, the coordination of work and agreement on targets becomes complex. One of the solutions to this type of project is to have a more complete view of the overall process, as in the Ways of Working. Remember that *Harvard Business Review* article that spoke of attaching yourself to an order. The problem has been that orders cross organizational lines. This is an easy task for the new graphics models.

Even when business process re-engineering is recommended by management, a major problem is encountered in developing a definition of requirements that each party agrees to and understands in the same way. When the requirements for the application system and the functional model that relates those requirements are referred to in the course of accomplishing tasks, it has been found that different interpretations can occur. The analysis of requirements problems was made during the analysis of systems re-engineering discussed earlier. Major firms have encountered problems when preparing a document to define requirements.

CONCLUSION

This new approach with implementation engineering models came about because a real need existed. The primary need was to implement complex systems in organizations that did not design them and for whom they were not originally designed. But to the CFO looking forward, they represent other notable opportunities. Because they are business process oriented, these tools, such as Ways of Working, can be used to satisfy regulatory requirements, provide solutions to board of director dictates for downsizing, outsourcing, and re-engineering, and contribute significantly to the improvement of productivity of information systems and user personnel alike.

Perhaps equally as important, the CFO can bridge that elusive gap of communication between users and information services technicians. As a *Computerworld* article claimed, CFOs can secure the sponsorship of top executives for critical information systems projects. In "Try Speaking English," several CEOs balked at ORBs, BAPIs, and APIs; they just wanted to define in a clear manner the costs, training needs, and implementation approach. Ways of Working is the answer.

This analysis leads to the need to take advantage of existing technologies in defining our processes for training, productivity, regulatory compliance, and business process re-engineering studies. It emphasizes the critical nature of the documentation process—that it be process-oriented, graphical, devisable into understandable segments, and iterative. This requirement extends to the design and implementation of proposed re-engineered processes. It follows quite logically to the operations, training, and continuous improvement of ongoing systems and business processes. It is the new implementation engineering approach of the 1990s—Ways of Working.

As we observed in the Foreword to this book, the approach is important in increasing information solution value, simplifying information systems management, and reducing information solution cost of ownership. In regard to improving information solution value, Ways of Working improves end-user productivity as well as improving the quality and value of technical and business process user communications. Regarding simplifying information systems management, these new implementation models provide viable and efficient maintenance of "living" system documentation in a single location. In addition, these tools support industry compliance standards including both internal and mandated FDA standards and facilitate business process change. Finally, in regard to reducing information solution cost of ownership, Ways of Working provides critical support for the rapid implementation methodology, reduces industry compliance and certification overhead, and ensures efficient business continuity. These observations were made by a real life user of one of these implementation models. Their capabilities are summarized as follows:

1. *Improving end-user productivity.* Ways of Working models provide multilevel contextual on-line help. Users can access descriptive flows by module or business process. Each level is supported by graphics and text and the processes decompose to work statements or desk procedures to help the users do their jobs more efficiently. Productivity improves with on-line help because users can help themselves through complex procedures rather than disrupting their neighbors and supervisors. In addition, these tools prove integrated on-line user training that will always be more efficient than classroom training and will always be there when the classroom instructor is long gone. Finally, productivity is improved by the availability and easy access to the appropriate standard operating procedure.

2. *Supporting business process improvement.* The key here is the visibility of the business process and the ability to link cross-divisional functions in a single viewing. Then, the CFO or user manager can simulate different alternatives and improve business processes since business participants contribute and redundancies become obvious. Combining current practices with best practices (such as the AMR supply chain model) the CFO can promote improvements in the business process and evaluate how similar companies do similar things. Finally, the ability to cost out different alternatives with activity-based costing provides the communication the CFO needs to justify change and support business process improvements. The costing, of course, also encourages "what if" dialog between the CFO and his or her constituents for the ultimate benefit of the enterprise.

3. *Adding strategic value to formerly tactical projects.* The tools literally generate "as is" and "to be" documentation so the benefits can be viewed, calculated, and communicated. Procedural errors can be seen before they become problems in actuality. Another value is the currency of the training and training materials, since the repository of user procedures can easily be made to be current. Incidentally, the strategic value is also enhanced by elimination of redundant systems documentation.

4. *Supporting workflow planning efforts.* Tracing documents with these implementation tools clearly streamlines the flow of work, the flow of documents, and the entire documentation management function.

5. *Improving the quality and value of communications among business and technical staffs.* This is so, for the simple but proven fact that both technicians and business staffs can understand the decomposition of systems to ever-increasing levels of detail, the simple icons that are used at the business process and the

procedural levels, and the visual presentation of each. Process flows, as shown in this book, are easily understood by both. Icons can be rectangles, circles, or actual presentations of the function (e.g., a question mark for a decision and a person for a job category, etc.).

The CFO can also benefit from the simplification of information systems management which is possible with this implementation approach. This is possible because of the following capabilities of these tools:

1. *Viable and efficient maintenance of "living" system documentation in a single location.* This means that all documentation of the enterprise relating to systems and supporting organizations can be resident in a single repository created and maintained by the implementation tool. Included here are the enterprise business flows, the business functional narratives, and job descriptions in the context of the business process.

2. *Productive approach to end-user support.* This is possible through the capability to develop business process-oriented on-line help and the integrated, on-line job function training and potential certification. The CFO can benefit from this type of support which users have sought since the inception of computer use but with which they have so seldom been provided.

3. *Supporting industry compliance.* This is so because the very heart of these tools is the repository of fully documented procedures and work statements in a single and easily accessible location. Experience has shown that the CFO does not have to redesign and document systems and procedures for ISO 9000 certification, for example, when they already exist in the enterprise repository for day-to-day operations. This is often abused by zealous consultants who come into a company on an ISO 9000 project and completely rewrite all relevant procedures. Users of implementation models will reference and access relevant procedures from the repository at significant savings and efficiency. There is no duplication of effort, redundant procedures, or consulting work, and therefore, these models support industry compliance.

4. *Business process change facilitation.* This is so because the impact of systems changes can be so easily viewed with the recommended visual presentation that is at the heart of these implementation models. In addition, dissemination of any new procedures to the ultimate end-user is facilitated. Remember, the approach recommended here is a repository of Ways of Working in the form of business processes and procedures that are retrievable on-line and accessible to all involved end-users. This facilitates the change process because of the undeniable access to current and proposed changes in the way we work. Finally, change is facilitated because the on-line repository facilitates continuing end-user education and training support. By defining work in terms of business processes (what to do) and detailed work statements or procedures (how we do it), the implementation tools provide a continuous training facility without the requirement to develop training courses, select and train a trainer, organize and furnish a classroom, and schedule trainer and trainee. In this important regard, the Ways of Working concept enhances the process and success rate of change.

Finally, this implementation approach, when used effectively, can be beneficial to the CFO by reducing the information solution cost of ownership. This is possible because of the following capabilities of these tools:

1. *Avoidance of redundant systems documentation efforts.* CFOs can eliminate redundancies because of the ease of maintaining this repository of systems and procedures. There is no need to make changes, update the text using a word processing system, print the changed process, bind it (or index it), and distribute to many offices. Here, documentation is maintained on-line and the network run-time version is updated internally for all central and remote users. This central repository, in itself, avoids the requirement for redundant systems documentation. In addition, the multiple views of the same processes and procedures eliminates the need for redundancy. These processes can be viewed:

   • Functionally

      a. Operations

      b. Regulatory Compliance

      c. Disaster Recovery Planning

   • Training

   • Organizationally

   Because of this capability, it should be obvious to visionary CFOs that they do not need to create and maintain multiple copies of the same procedures for each function, training session, or human resource record retention requirement.

2. *Reducing audit fees.* A major cost of the annual audit is the documentation of business processes and identification of internal controls. The implementation approach provides the format and visibility to focus auditors and pinpoint processes, internal controls, and management controls. The resulting benefit is, of course, to reduce the time (and billable hours) required to complete the audit. The public accounting firm may balk in the first year but literally have no argument in subsequent years. Auditing is now considered by most to be a commodity; this repository of internal processes and procedures enhances and furthers that position.

3. *Reducing end-user support burden.* This is due to the detail of documentation in the Ways of Working methodology. Overall support and training of new and temporary employees is greatly enhanced by these implementation tools. Temporary employees are usually trained by the nearest employee who is knowledgeable. This effort is significantly reduced by this business process repository.

4. *Providing critical support for rapid implementation methodology.* The repository can easily support the use and modification of best practices predefined business processes. This was demonstrated in real life and reported herein with the SCOR (Supply Chain Operations reference model) project for Advanced Management Research in Boston. The repository, as we have discussed, shortens the education and training cycles, thus supporting rapid implementation. The visionary CFO recognizes that training is one of the key elements in the systems development life cycle and one of the longer term projects impacting the speed of implementation projects and their success. Equally as important in support of the rapid implementation methodology is the efficient knowledge transfer from outside consultants to in-house

user staff. The repository, in a standard enterprise-wide format, can be understood and communicated quite clearly, as we have shown throughout this book.

5. *Ensuring efficient business continuity.* This continuity is a reflection on the advantages of seeing the entire enterprise and its business processes visually. Incidentally, this argument for use of the implementation approach is also propagated by software vendors in addressing the issue of protecting your software investment. In addition, business continuity is improved by the earlier productivity of new employees that is possible with accurate Ways of Working documentation.

6. *Eliminating some start-up costs in future migratory planning and execution efforts.* These models or tools, have in the past, been referred to as "delta" products in that they can clearly define the "before" and "after" or "as is" and "to be" scenarios. To begin with, the "as is" is always documented as a reference point. The "to be" is easier to document from this perspective than from the blank paper perspective. Changes can be highlighted, color-coded, and explained through creative use of changing icons. The significance of this cost will not be lost on the visionary CFO and the effect on the bottom line will be visible to executive management.

Critical questions that can be posed to a CFO are as follows:

- The next time you plan to enhance your information solution, will you have to start with an "as is" assessment and procedural documentation project?
- Do your information systems staff all think and operate in terms of how your business works and how the business benefits from a productive information systems solution?
- Are FDA, ISO 9000, or other regulatory requirements a business objective or a marketing necessity for you and your enterprise?
- Do you agree with your end-users that they require more available and sophisticated support in their day-to-day operations?
- Do the same support and educational or training issues constantly recur?
- Do you believe that your annual enterprise-wide information and internal control audits are too costly and unnecessarily distracting to your staff?
- When the annual audit or product validation issues and projects come up, do you feel that you and your staff are reinventing the wheel on each occasion?
- Are the maintenance, currency, redundancy, availability, and visuality of user procedures and corresponding training materials a problem for you and your enterprise?

If you are like many others, the answers to many (if not all) of these questions is a resounding yes.

The solution is at hand through the effort required to define your Ways of Working. Through implementation of this concept, imbedded in new implementation engineering models and tools, we predict with a great amount of certainty and experience that you will find increasing information solution value, simplification of information systems management, and a real reduction in the cost of ownership of the information systems function.

A Typical Process Definition: Defining Our Ways of Working

The sequence of screens is presented on the following pages.

Process:
Courtesy of Ross Online Knowledge
Delivered through the Strategic Application Modeler (SAM) product
Ross Systems, Inc., 1997
Atlanta, Georgia

FIGURE A.1
Business Knowledge Repository Gateway

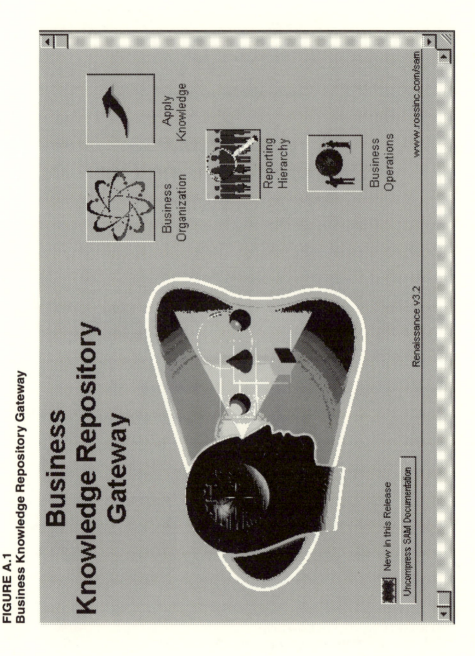

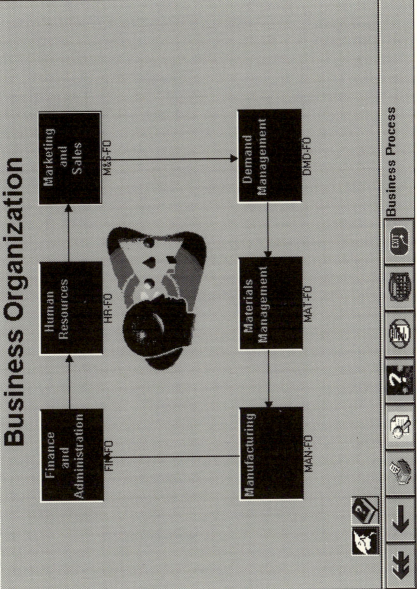

FIGURE A.3
Materials Management

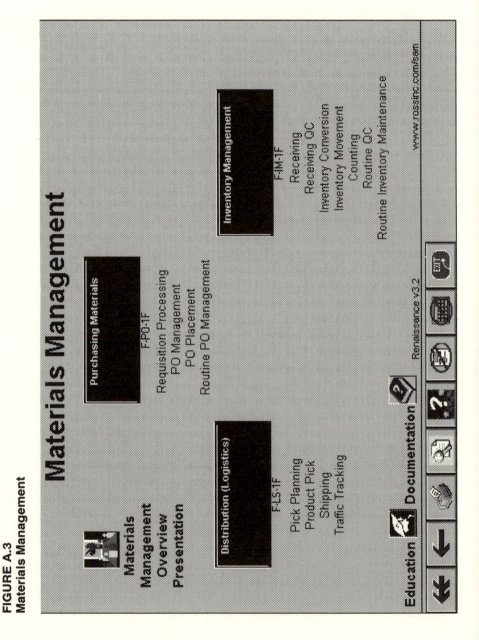

FIGURE A.4
Purchasing Materials

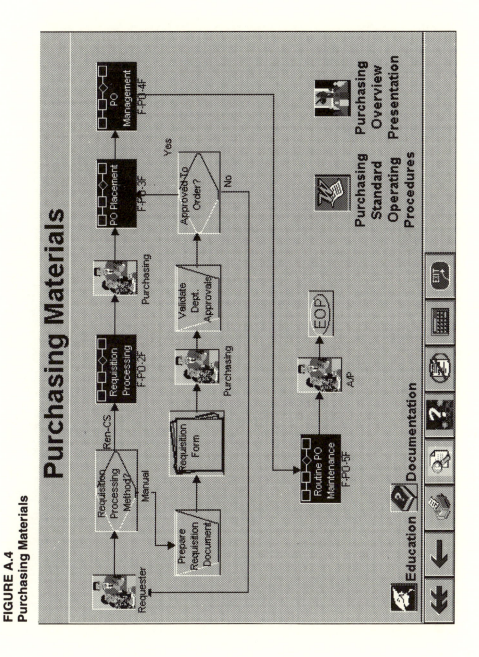

FIGURE A.5
Requisition Processing

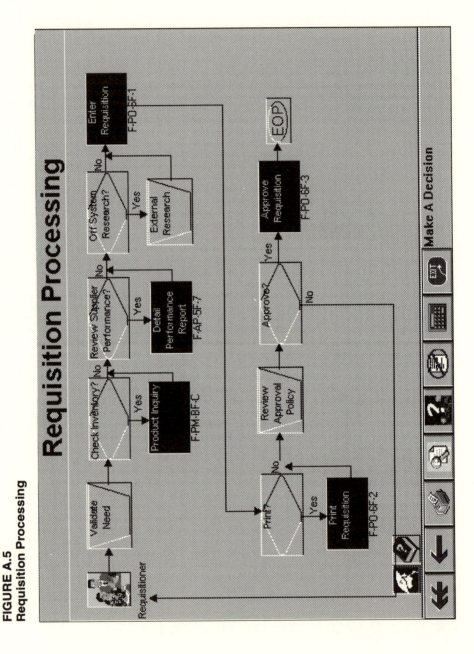

Requisition Processing

FIGURE A.6
Requisition Entry

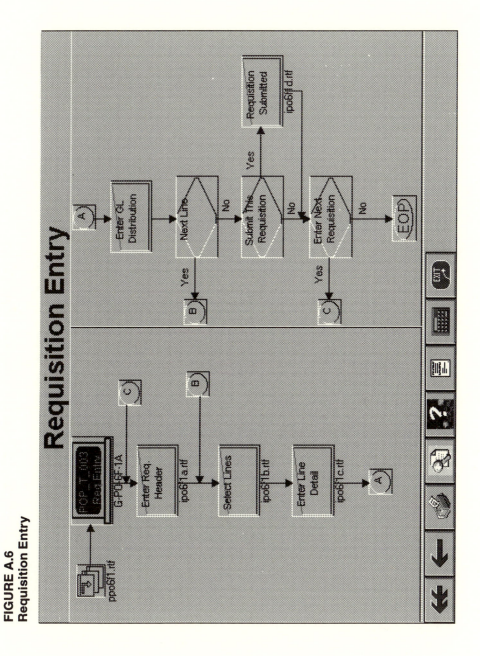

Requisition Entry

POP T 003 Req Entry

ppo6f1.rtf

G-PO6F-1A

Enter Req. Header — ipo6f1a.rtf

Select Lines — ipo6f1b.rtf

Enter Line Detail — ipo6f1c.rtf

Enter GL Distribution

Next Line — No / Yes → B

Submit This Requisition — No / Yes → Requisition Submitted — ipo6ff d.rtf

Enter Next Requisition — No / Yes → C → EOP

A

Index

ABOUT THE AUTHORS

JUD BRESLIN is President of the COBRE Group, Inc., a Morristown, New Jersey, consultancy firm that designs, implements, and manages software systems in a variety of industries for various applications. Before founding his firm, Breslin held positions with Touche Ross and Cresap McCormick & Paget, and was also Deputy Administrator for the U.S. Energy Office. He holds an MBA from the Wharton School and is the author of several books, including *Selecting and Installing Software Packages* (Quorum, 1986).

JOHN McGANN has been in charge of information technology planning at Allied Chemical and American Airlines. He has also been a Vice President of Systems Planning at Chase Bank and an MIS Director for the New York City Finance Administration., With degrees from MIT and Columbia University, he has been Adjunct Professor of Computing Science and has lectured on information technology planning at other universities and at various conferences. McGann performs consulting services and prepares reports on various information technology matters for companies including IBM, Microsoft, Unisys, Chase, and Bank America.

ISBN 0-89930-484-2

90000>

EAN

9 780899 304847

HARDCOVER BAR CODE